HIDDEN HISTORY *of* TERRE HAUTE

HIDDEN HISTORY *of* TERRE HAUTE

Tim Crumrin

THE History PRESS

Published by The History Press
Charleston, SC
www.historypress.com

Cover image of Lou Johnson courtesy of Vigo County Historical Society.

First published 2020

Manufactured in the United States

ISBN 9781467146135

Library of Congress Control Number: 2020934342

Dedicated to all my little ones over all the years, for all they bring to my life.

Contents

Acknowledgements

No book of history is the product of the author alone. Many others contribute. In this book, I have been fortunate to have had so many who aided and encouraged me along the way.

As always, the staffs of the Special Collections Department of the Vigo County Public Library and the Indiana State University Archives made the author feel welcome and were unstinting in their efforts to provide whatever materials were needed to support my research.

The thorough work of Vigo County Historian Mike McCormick provided a solid starting point and clarification to many of the chapters in this book.

My sincere thanks to my acquisitions editor at The History Press, John Rodrigue, who once again shepherded this work with his skills and understanding.

I cannot emphasize enough my gratitude for the support of the staff and volunteers of the Vigo County Historical Society. Marylee Hagen, Tanis Nicklasch and Susan Tingley were ever helpful, all while working to open the county's magnificent new museum. I wish to particularly thank Susan Tingley for suggesting several topics that appear in these pages.

To my great-niece, Lylah Crumrin, who more than once pointed out that her sister's name appeared in one of my previous books but not hers, I say… here you are, Lylah Marie.

On the homefront, my daughter, Brynn, and grandchildren Tanner, Kyle and Daisey (mostly) understood that the book sometimes had to take precedent over going to the movies or swimming.

And, as always, to my wife, Robin Rohrkaste Crumrin.

Introduction

All towns have their hidden stories—some barely remembered, some unknown and some willingly forgotten. Terre Haute, Indiana, is the same. This book tells a wide range of those hidden histories, from sports to entertainment, from disasters to crimes and from innovators to those on the edges of society. How many know that Terre Haute once had two motion picture studios and was a center of aircraft innovation or that a product of the Wabash River was once *the* haute couture item in fashionable Paris?

Or that it can be said that Terre Haute was the epicenter of the soda pop business? That the most famous college basketball coach of all time first bestrode the college hardwood in the city? That two very different women conquered the worlds of art and entertainment?

Here, too, are the darker stories of the death cry of the gypsy and a man lynched from a bridge.

The hidden history of Terre Haute is no longer so hidden.

INNOVATION

THE SKIES ABOVE TERRE HAUTE

Terre Haute was home to two significant events in airplane design in the United States. In the decade after Kitty Hawk, it is estimated that two thousand people across the country tried their hands at building planes. Almost all followed the Wright brothers' biplane designs—but not the Johnson brothers.

The work of the four brothers from Terre Haute, who succeeded in making the first successful monoplane flight in the United States in 1911, was innovative. The Wright brothers led to the biplane era, but the Johnson brothers' experiments would show the ultimate superiority of the monoplane and lead to the modern era of flight.

Louis, Julius, Harry and Clarence Johnson were the redheaded sons of Danish immigrant Soren Johnson and his wife, Bertha. Soren Johnson immigrated to the United States as a young boy in 1855. He eventually became a blacksmith and settled in Terre Haute. His mechanical skills were passed on to his inventive sons.

Louis, the oldest son, was a naturally inventive young man. He built his own sled when his parents told him that they could not afford to buy one. When he and his brothers wanted a boat, they were told to build one—so they did. Tired of rowing the eighteen-foot boat miles upstream to harvest walnuts, Lou looked for a better idea. It was then that the Johnson boys began tinkering with engines. In doing so, they found their calling. The brothers began building a marine engine in 1904. They soon were building and selling inline marine engines. Many felt that they were superior to other models available at the time. A boat equipped with a Johnson motor could attain a speed of eighteen miles per hour.

In 1908, with the backing of the Terre Haute Chamber of Commerce, they built a factory at Sixteenth and Hulman Streets in Terre Haute. They continued to look for other adaptive uses for their engines. They soon started adding them to bicycles and sold more than 2,500 motorbikes before 1920. Business was good.

Powered flight became a mania among many following the Wright brothers' historic flight at Kitty Hawk. Newspapers of the era trumpeted each new flight development and lionized early pilots. The Terre Haute newspapers were no different, as they often featured breathless accounts about the daring men (and sometimes women) from around the world who conquered the air. The Johnson brothers were entranced at the thought of building airplane engines. They studied the mechanics of the Wright brothers' early flying machines. Their experience with engines and speed led them to conceive the idea of building their own plane. Their plane, however, would be different from those of others. Harry Johnson later recalled that one of the brothers had seen a picture of the monoplane that Frenchman Louis Blériot flew across the English Channel in 1909. The idea of a single-wing plane intrigued them.

The brothers began serious work on the plane during the spring of 1910, testing out the engine and assembly designs. They settled on the monoplane model. It had a wood frame with silk-covered wings. During the first week of August, they moved the plane to a field near Black Hawk, southeast of Terre Haute. Wishing to keep their tests secret, they erected tents, but word soon got out and locals flocked to the area to see what it was all about. They spent two months testing all the elements of their design. Failures were followed by a meticulous reworking of the design. The brothers had no plans for a sustained flight. They wanted to test the machine. Their engine hit forty horsepower, and they were sure that they could squeeze out another twenty if they pushed it. They paid special attention to the wheels, as they worried they were too light to handle the strain of liftoff and landings. Finally, their creation (weighing 750 pounds, with a thirty-six-foot wingspan) was ready for the test. After two attempts, Louis Johnson revved the engine and moved slowly down the farm field in the gathering dusk of Sunday, October 9. The plane

A proud Lou Johnson standing in front of the monoplane. *Vigo County Historical Society*.

lifted about a foot off the ground and "flew" about twenty feet. The crew and pilot rejoiced.

To those who wondered why the flight was not higher and longer, Louis Johnson explained that they were mainly trying to test the buoyancy, balance and strength of their invention. They disassembled the plane and returned to their factory. Due to the curiosity of the public, the engine was displayed in the window of a Terre Haute department store.

After mulling over the results, the Johnsons decided to use tubular steel for the frame and wings. That would make the plane lighter and stronger. It would also make it easier to assemble or dismantle the aircraft. Worried

Lou in flight. *Vigo County Historical Society.*

about the stress on the propeller and drive shafts, they tinkered with those and felt that the new construction would ease the strain on those vital parts of the plane. They announced that their next plane would be made entirely of tubular steel and plane fabric. The brothers planned to take it to an undisclosed location in the South to test their new ideas over the winter. The new design had no cockpit. The pilot sat on a band of canvas with no seatbelts. Harry had carved the propeller out of spruce and walnut.

By the following August, they were ready to try again. Moving the plane to a farm north of Terre Haute, they made history. Lou was the neophyte pilot and admitted, "When that plane was ready to go up I had not the remotest idea how to fly." At 5:00 a.m., on August 8, 1911, they powered up their engine, and Louis Johnson rolled down the field. After trundling about one hundred feet, Lou was four feet aloft over the west-central Indiana landscape. On its second flight, the plane "behaved perfectly," and Lou took it up to forty feet for three hundred yards. He later said he was too busy to be scared.

The air was smooth, no turbulence, so Lou decided to try gliding. He shut off the engine and glided until making a perfect landing. The Johnson brothers had succeeded in making the first sustained flight of a monoplane in U.S. history.

The news electrified flying circles. More tinkering made the plane even better, and the Johnsons were soon demonstrating their plane at fairs

Barnstorming ad. *Vigo County Historical Society.*

and exhibitions throughout Indiana, sometimes making $2,500 per weekend. Lou especially liked racing railroad trains. Occasionally, the engineers would simply stop the trains to allow passengers to get out and watch and wave at Lou and his monoplane.

One of their exhibitions almost didn't get off the ground. They were scheduled to fly one weekend in Arthur, Illinois. The problem was that Arthur was Amish country. Local farmers refused to allow the brothers to use their fields to showcase their newfangled motor-driven plane to soil their property. It seemed that the exhibition was off until a man pushed his way through the crowd. He was an Amish "outcast" who had shaved his beard and distanced himself from the community. He offered his field for the flight. The curiosity of the crowds overcame their views on modern conveniences, and they followed as the brothers set up the plane in the new field. Women gathered around with their parasols. Julius Johnson shouted, "Watch out. I'm starting the motor. Close your parasols." His advice went unheeded. As the engine sparked to life, horses shied and kicked at their traces, and the air was filled with floating parasols.

Their fame spread, and the brothers' dream of operating a successful engine and plane building firm seemed ready to take flight. Orders poured into their Terre Haute factory. But in a heartbreakingly ironic twist, those who had "conquered" the air became its victim. On Easter Sunday, March 23, 1913, a horrendous tornado swept through the Terre Haute area. Scores were killed. Among the businesses flattened by the twister, the Johnson factory was literally torn from its foundation and carried off on the turbulent winds. Thoughts of airplane building ended. Their monoplane was abandoned in a farm field near Terre Haute, left to time's ravages.

Although that was the end of their airplane business, the brothers carried on. They rebuilt their plant, this time concentrating on engine-building. They entered their four-cylinder engine in a competition in Mineola, New York, in 1915. It outclassed all the others by running ten hours without missing a stroke. They were hoping to interest the American government in buying their engines for its fledgling flying corps, but no sales were forthcoming. One government was interested though. Representatives of Czarist Russia approached the brothers about making airplane engines for them. However, the Russians wanted a twelve-cylinder engine. The brothers tried to meet the requirements but couldn't find a magneto powerful enough to reliably work in the ignition system. Had the Russians offered an "experimental contract" to allow more time for tinkering, Harry Johnson felt they could have ultimately provided the requested engine. But the Russians declined, and the Johnson decided to concentrate on their first love: marine engines.

Seeing the Johnson brothers,' success, the City of South Bend, Indiana, lured them with a promise of a new factory. There and later in Waukegan, Illinois, Johnson Brothers Motor Company began building outboard motors for boats. Eventually, the firm would join with the Evinrude Company to manufacture the famous Johnson-Evinrude engines.

Although the Johnson brothers' successful experiments with flight were short-lived, they were among the most important pioneers in America's quest to conquer the air. Their all-metal monoplanes were the prototypes of the future, when the wood-and-canvas, multi-winged era gave way to the modern era. Their status as groundbreakers was confirmed in 1959 when the Smithsonian mounted a special exhibit about their work that included a scale model of their monoplane overseen by Harry Johnson and a feature on the brothers in its magazine.

Argosy magazine celebrated the Johnson brothers on the fiftieth anniversary of their first flight. It lamented that others did not build on the brothers' work: "Who knows how the course of aviation would have gone by now if only someone had followed the lead of the Johnson brothers, who designed a fabulous, streamlined airplane twenty-five years too soon."

The Natural-Born Mechanic

The Johnson brothers' exploits inspired others, among them a young man named Gus Riggs. Born in Shelburn, Indiana, in 1888, he moved to Terre Haute with his family as a young man. Still, years later, locals in Sullivan County remembered young Gus as a "natural born mechanic" and how "no piece of machinery would prove too intricate for him."

After seeing Orville Wright piloting one of his and Wilbur's biplanes in Indianapolis in 1910 and learning of the Johnson brothers' efforts, Riggs was determined to step onto the path they were blazing. He eagerly followed the Johnsons' progress and witnessed many of their flights.

Riggs started to experiment with design concepts in late 1911. He studied other designers' planes, adopting elements from different aircraft. Riggs began building his first plane in 1912, but it was not of his design. His first plane was commissioned by a Terre Haute dentist named Belden. Dr. Belden wanted Gus to build him a replica of the latest Wright brothers' plane. Riggs found an owner of a Wright plane in St. Louis who allowed him to study it. He carefully measured and sketched out the plane. With drawings in hand, he returned to Terre Haute and got down to work. The aircraft was completed in early 1913 and ready for its first flight. As it rumbled down the farm field serving as a runway, Gus Riggs must have been proud and excited. The plane took flight but then stalled and crashed. It was not rebuilt.

Despite the "failure" of his first venture, Riggs was not deterred. After all, it was someone else's design, and it was an engine problem—not a fault in the construction.

Gus Riggs in front of his tractor plane. *Vigo County Historical Society.*

Riggs then went back to working on his own plane. What he finally decided on was another great innovation in American aviation history. Riggs built what many—though not all—feel was the first "tractor airplane" in the nation. A tractor plane was one that had both the propeller and engine in front of the pilot, instead of behind or beside the intrepid aviators. Riggs felt that this was much safer for the pilot.

The plane was made of spruce and ash with a twenty-two-foot wingspan. Riggs claimed that the wood had been salvaged from a coffin. But unlike the Johnson brothers, he chose to follow the biplane design of the Wright brothers. In fact, his first model was a nearly exact replica of the latest Wright plane. The propeller was made by an engineering student at Rose Polytechnic and measured more than eight feet. Obviously, Riggs was not superstitious, as the engine—a ninety-horsepower, eight-cylinder Hall-Scott—had been salvaged from the wreck of a plane that had crashed into the Pacific. Riggs named the plane *13* for luck because he started building it on the thirteenth of the month.

By June 1913, Riggs's plane had made nearly forty sustained flights, one of which was a nearly half-hour flight over Terre Haute. Across the city, people looked up at the plane soaring about four hundred feet above them. The air age was firmly planted in Terre Haute.

Riggs's next innovation was to add a passenger seat. Within six weeks, he was carrying fellow pilots and mechanics aloft with him. There was talk that he was going to take a camera up on a flight to film the damage done by the 1913 tornado and flood that destroyed the Johnson brothers' factory, but nothing came of it. Like the Johnsons, he took his plane for exhibition flights around the area. Also like the Johnsons, he gave up on building aircraft and spent many years as a plane designer.

Word of Riggs's skills spread. He went to work as a chief designer for the Weeks-Larson Aeroplane Company in Iowa in 1915. The plane they built became known as the Weeks-Rigg (sometimes referred to as Riggs-Wehr) model. The next year, he was in New York working for the Standard Aeroplane Company. In 1916, he was hired by the Curtiss Aeroplane Company, founded by aviation legend Glenn Curtiss.

With U.S. entry into World War I, Riggs fervently wanted to "get in the war game." Congressman Everett Sanders, who served Riggs's district in Indiana, recommended him for appointment to the U.S. Aviation Service as an expert in aircraft manufacturing. One of the jobs in the technical service was to oversee quality control of aircraft sold to the armed forces. Riggs was accepted and sent back to Curtiss as an inspector in August 1917.

Riggs's crew readies plane. *Vigo County Historical Society*.

He really got into the war game in 1918 when he was commissioned as a lieutenant and assigned to the Aerial Corps in Italy. There and later in France, he oversaw airplane maintenance. His mechanical skills were especially invaluable in areas like adapting American guns so they could be fitted onto French warplanes.

He returned to Terre Haute after the war. In 1919, partnering with the Hearst Airplane Company of Terre Haute, he designed a commercial aircraft that he called the most powerful plane yet built. Power was the key to the plane, not speed, as it was meant to haul freight. He also tried his hand at automobiles, building a custom-designed car for a local auto enthusiast. He spent the next decade working as a designer for aircraft companies in Oklahoma. Gus Riggs moved on from aviation to other businesses in the 1930s. His only other involvement with aviation came during World War II. He was commissioned a major in administration in the U.S. Army Air Corps. He died in 1962.

Like the Johnson brothers, Gus Riggs pioneered innovations that advanced the evolution of aircraft.

SODA POP'S POP

Everybody said that Jacob Baur would "make his way in the world." He was bright and energetic and described by a local newspaper as "one of the boys who is all grit." They could not know then that he would become the "Father of the Soda Fountain" and one of the most important people in the history of the soda pop business.

A second-generation pharmacist, Baur reportedly graduated first in his class from the Philadelphia College of Pharmacy in 1881 and returned to Terre Haute to rejoin the family business. The Baur drugstore, located at Seventh and Wabash, was like any other pharmacy. It sold various patent medicines said to cure everything from bronchitis to erectile dysfunction. Rheumatism was the affliction suffered by many of its customers, so it carried at least five nostrums advertised as cures for "the Tiz." He also mixed and sold prescriptions and other drugs, including heroin, morphine and cocaine, which were legal at the time.

Baur was always looking for ways to increase business. He started carrying more items to interest their female customers. He and his brother, Charles, concocted "Lettuce Lotion" in their lab at the back of the store. It was marketed as the cure for sensitive, rough skin. They also proudly announced that they sold Prairie Queen perfumes.

The fall of 1881 brought a man to Terre Haute who would forever alter Jacob Baur's life. Adolph Convert was young man from Strasbourg, Germany, who held a doctorate in chemistry. How he wound his way to Terre Haute is unknown, but he was "green in American ways" and wanted to learn more about his new home. He took a series of temporary jobs as he traveled the country. After appearing in Terre Haute, he accepted the rather lowly job as a drug clerk at the Baur store. He and Jacob became good friends.

Like at many drugstores, the Baurs made and sold soda water, but it was costly and difficult to make. They needed large brass tanks of water into which they mixed "sulfuric acid and marble dust to charge [carbonate] the water." This method also left traces of arsenic in the "mineral water." While sitting around the drugstore's lab, Convert and Jacob discussed the chemical process for making soda water. When Convert told him that chemists in Germany were working on a method of liquifying carbonic gas so it could be transported in small tanks, Baur was intrigued.

It is likely that he and Convert began experimenting with different methods of making soda water. In 1882, a Terre Haute paper noted the Baurs had "blowed in" their new soda fountain but gave no further explanation. Whether that meant there was some sort of accident due to Jacob's experiments is not clear. In any case, while on a ten-week tour of Europe the next spring, Jacob Baur went to Germany to check out the chemists Convert had told him about and study their methods.

Birthplace of the soda fountain. Baur's Drug Store, 1907. *Vigo County Historical Society.*

Baur continued his experiments upon his return. It took five long years of experimentation in his lab, but in 1886, he succeeded in his quest. Baur finally came up with a way to "liquify" carbon dioxide. This ability to put his "liquid" carbonic acid into pressurized containers was nothing short of revolutionary. It would forever change how carbonated beverages were made. It allowed druggists and others to make their own carbonated beverages at a much lower cost. In essence, Jacob Baur invented the soda fountain, a phenomenon that still exists today. He was the "King of the Soda Fountain."

Realizing the potential of his discovery, Baur began soliciting investment money from wealthy Terre Haute friends and formed the Liquid Carbonic Acid Manufacturing Company in 1888. At first, the company manufactured small tanks of carbonic acid locally and sold them to druggists. Soon the company was flourishing. Within six years, the company had set up manufacturing plants in Pittsburgh, Chicago and St. Louis. This only fed the demand for its product. Eventually, it had offices in eleven cities, including New York, Dallas and Atlanta, home of the Coca-Cola Company. Soda fountain owners, breweries and bottling plants clamored for the product.

But Jacob Baur was not satisfied with just supplying carbonic acid. By 1900, his company was in the business of manufacturing soda fountains. Its fountains became the industry standard, the best that could be purchased. Liquid Carbonic continued to refine and add to its product. It added the Liquid Iceless Soda Fountain, which used "ammonia gas" as its coolant. It produced its first electricity-powered fountain that could produce twenty gallons of carbonated water per day.

The company became the one-stop-shopping business for anyone wishing to add a soda fountain. It could provide the fountain, glassware and any utensil needed for a successful operation. It did not stop there. It also offered syrups for making fruit drinks and other concoctions, such as Cherry Punch and "Nut Confections."

In the early years, it was even thought that the gas could be used as "motive power for horseless carriages." On an 1897 visit to Terre Haute, Baur boasted that inventors were experimenting with it as a fuel. Sadly, nothing came of the idea.

After a quarter century of traveling the world to sell his "invention" and creating a new industry, Jacob Baur died in Chicago of complications of a heart condition. Announcing his death, a Terre Haute newspaper called him "Terre Haute's richest native son."

Baur's spawning of a beverage industry and Terre Haute serving as the "Birthplace of the Coke Bottle" made the city the epicenter of the soft drink revolution.

The Sportin' Life

The Garfield Olympians

Garfield High School, on Terre Haute's northside, often had to play second string to its main city rivals. Gerstmeyer Tech had the consistently stronger basketball program, while Wiley was usually a football power. But there was one area where Garfield Purple Eagles surpassed them all: the Olympic Games. Former Garfield athletes won gold medals in three consecutive Olympics from 1952 to 1960.

The first was big Clyde Lovellette in 1952. Lovellette was the first of the "man mountain" centers in college basketball. Unlike the slender big men of the era such as George Mikan and Bob Kurland, Clyde was six-foot-nine and weighed over 240 pounds. He had the bulk to dominate the middle but also became an adept mid-range shooter.

What Clyde initially lacked was agility and the proper footwork. Taking a cue from DePaul coach Ray Meyer's transformation of Mikan, Lovellette's Garfield coach, Willard Kehrt, had Big Clyde take up dancing to improve his coordination. Clyde spent hours dancing with his mother and sister in the family's backyard. Although he found it embarrassing, he kept at it. His terpsichorean training, along with jumping rope and shadow boxing, greatly improved his game. By his senior year, he was the most sought-after big man in the Midwest.

Naturally, many Terre Haute fans wanted him to head down to Bloomington to play under Coach Branch McCracken at Indiana

University. Lovellette did commit to IU, but wily (some said crooked) Kansas coach Phog Allen swept in at the last minute. Just as Clyde was packing to head to Bloomington, Allen rolled up in his Cadillac and basically snatched Lovellette from his porch and drove back to Kansas, his prize big man in the seat beside him.

Clyde found glory at Kansas. He was a two-time consensus All-American and was named the College Player of the Year in 1952. He led the Jayhawks to the 1952 NCAA Championship. (McCracken's Hurryin' Hoosiers won it the following year.) There was one more challenge ahead for him in 1952.

The U.S. Olympic basketball team was selected differently during Lovellette's era. NCAA champions competed against Amateur Athletic Union (AAU) teams in the tourney. Two powerhouse AAU teams, the Caterpillar Diesels and Phillips 66ers, were also in the tourney. The 66ers featured 1948 gold medal winner Bob Kurland on the team. Kansas played the Diesels for the championship but lost, 62–60, as Lovellette missed a last-second shot to tie the game. The Diesels' coach, the alliteratively named Warren Womble, thus became Olympic team head coach and selected the roster, which included five Diesels, Bob Kurland and another 66er and seven Kansas players. Clyde Lovellette was going to the Olympics.

The Olympics were held in Helsinki, Finland, with Bob Kurland as flag bearer. Wearing a blue jacket, gray slacks and a red, white and blue tie, Lovellette walked proudly through the rain-soaked opening ceremony. Then it was time for the games to begin.

The specter of the Cold War hung over the 1952 Olympics. Although the rest of the athletes mingled freely in the Olympic village, the Soviets and their forced East Bloc allies were in their own compound. Armed guards surrounded the compound, and the athletes ate separately and were not supposed to mingle with other competitors. There was even a rumor, easy to believe considering Stalin's paranoia, that there were official food-tasters to prevent poisoning of the "red" athletes.

The basketball venue was crude. The games were played outdoors on a raised court. Lovellette quickly learned that the winds could affect his shots. The year 1952 was the first time the Soviet Union sent a basketball team, and Lovellette felt that they were testing themselves against the American squad. Both teams went 3-0 in group play to advance to the round robin medal round.

The U.S. team beat the Russians handily in their first encounter. The two teams met again in the gold medal game, during which Clyde Lovellette nearly caused an international incident. Late in the first half, Clyde reached in to slap away the ball from the Russian center (the ball was smaller and more slippery that American basketballs). The ball squirted away. Fearing that the Russian would grab the ball for a layup, Lovellette thought that his only recourse was to kick the ball out of bounds. As he kicked, the Russian center went for the ball. What followed was a sickening sound like a "coconut splitting."

Lovellette had split the opponent's hand between the ring and middle fingers. Blood spurted onto the court as the Soviet bloc fans lustily booed Big Clyde. For a moment, it seemed that a "rumble in the stands" was imminent, as some spectators looked like they were about to rush the court. Immediately, U.S. wrestlers and boxers stood up to join a possible melee. Lovellette was pulled from the court.

As there was little time left in the half, the referees wisely decided to call the end of the half. Boos greeted Lovellette as he made his second half appearance. The rest of the game was played without a major incident. It was hardly an artistic game. Lovellette called the 36–25 U.S. win a "terrible game." But as the horn sounded, the first of the Garfield Olympians had earned a gold medal.

The next Purple Eagle to win gold was Lovellette's classmate Greg Bell, a black man whose route to the Olympics was much more circuitous. Bell was born into a farm family just south of Terre Haute. Times were more than hard for the Bells. When their house burned down, Bell, his parents and nine siblings were forced to live in a chicken barn for twelve years. Bell never thought that sports would be a key to his future. Bell later noted that although he was always running around as a kid, he knew he was too short for basketball and too light for football. He didn't even know track and field was a sport until the family moved to Terre Haute and he attended Garfield. There he was encouraged to try track and ended up setting the school long jump records.

Bell thought that his sports career ended with his graduation. He went to work on a farm and did some factory work. He enlisted in the army in 1950, where officers saw his athletic potential. He was the long jump champion at the European Armed Forces Championships. With the end of his enlistment, he assumed that his sports career was again over.

However, a local physician named William Bannon kept pushing Bell to attend his alma mater, Indiana University, to study and continue long jumping. At IU, he began to dominate the long jump world. He would win three national AAU championships and two NCAA championships and be named an All-American three times.

Greg Bell (*left*) and Terry Dischinger (*third from left, seated*). *Vigo County Historical Society.*

He was chosen for the 1956 Olympic team in Melbourne, Australia. On November 24, he leaped 25.8 feet to take the gold medal. He felt that he could have done better, but the track was soft and he was jumping into the wind. He noted that he and fellow U.S. jumper and silver medalist John Bennett were a bit hampered because the runway to the jump was only 125 feet compared to the usual 150 feet.

For the next two years, he was the greatest long jumper in the world, winning gold in tournaments across the United States and the world. Bell was selected as an alternate for the 1960 games. After his Olympic win, he predicted that someone would break the 27-foot barrier soon given the right conditions. This was proven true five years later when Ralph Boston finally reached that milestone. He could not have foreseen that twelve years after his gold medal, Bob Beamon would soar past the 28-foot barrier and shock the world with his 29-foot, 2.66-inch jump.

Terry Dischinger was the best all-around athlete of the Garfield trio. He was a first baseman on the Terre Haute team that won the 1955 Babe Ruth World Series, was an end on the football team and a hurdler in track. He was also a straight-A student. But it was the basketball court where he dominated. He was six-foot-five and already an agile player as

Vigo County Historical Society.

a sophomore. By the time he graduated, he was six-foot-eight, a prolific scorer and an excellent defender and rebounder. He was the first athlete to twice win the MacMillan Award, given to the outstanding athlete in Vigo County.

He went to Purdue and quickly became the star on the basketball team. He averaged more than twenty-eight points per game in his Purdue career and, like Lovellette, was a two-time consensus All-American.

He was chosen for the 1960 Olympic Basketball team after his sophomore season. He joined what was arguably the best amateur basketball team in history. His teammates included Oscar Robertson, Jerry Lucas, Walt Bellamy and Jerry West. That team obliterated its opponents in the Rome Olympics. It averaged 101 points per game and averaged a 42.4-point victory margin. It beat Japan, 125–66. Dischinger and his teammates beat Brazil, 90–63, to win their gold medals.

The Rome Olympics became known as the Games that changed the world. It was the Olympics of Cassius Clay (Muhammad Ali) and Wilma Rudolph and Rafer Johnson. It was the first Games to be televised commercially, which only added to its popularity around the world. It also had several less welcome firsts. Rome in 1960 saw its first doping scandal when a Danish cyclist died during his race. The cause of his death was

Lovellette winning the tipoff at the 1947 state championship game. *Vigo County Historical Society*.

determined to be a reaction to the performance-enhancing drugs he had taken prior to the race. The gender of some female athletes was challenged and led to gender testing for athletes. Commercialization reared its head when it was discovered that Puma and Adidas had paid German athletes to wear their shoes.

The "shoe wars" started due to the feud between the German brothers Adolph and Rudolph Dassler, who had a shoemaking business. They were early members of the Nazi Party, and their business grew due to supplying shoes during the 1936 Olympics. Adolph became a coach and supplier of athletic shoes to the Hitler Youth. The brothers turned on each other after the war, each trying to prove that the other was the one most closely allied with the Nazis. Eventually, they split the company. Adolph's firm became Adidas, Rudolph founded Puma and the shoe war was on.

Four-Cornered Racetrack

Next to baseball, harness racing was arguably the second-most popular sport in late nineteenth-century America. It was considered far superior to Thoroughbred racing and the unsavory characters that sport attracted. One need only remember Professor Harold Hill's warning to the good citizens of River City: "Not a wholesome trottin' race, no, but a race where they set down right on the horse. Like to see some struck-up jockey boy sittin' on Dan Patch? Make your blood boil?"

The first harness races in Terre Haute may have been contested as early as 1859. A half-mile track was built in 1867 in conjunction with the Indiana State Fair, hosted that year by Terre Haute. That same year, Terre Haute mover and shaker Joseph Gilbert led the effort to build a one-mile oval track. It soon became a success, and a series of stake races were held over the years until more than $50,000 in purses were offered. Needless to say, it drew competitors from throughout the area. But in 1886, a new track was built, one that would make Terre Haute one of the most important destinations in harness racing for two decades.

The famous Four-Cornered Track was born. Its unusual shape was simply a matter of trying to fit the track into the available land. Due to the angle of the National Road (later Wabash Avenue) on the southern border of the tract, it was impossible to build the standard oval-shaped track. When a group of sportswriters first visited the track, they predicted that it would be

Four-Cornered Track. *Vigo County Historical Society.*

the fastest in the country. They were right. The long straightaways led to record after record.

Oddly, one of the first race meetings was for Thoroughbreds. The horses plodded through an incredibly muddy track. But harness racing was always king. Nearly every meeting resulted in one record or another. The first record was broken in 1889. A trotter named Axtell set two records in one race—one for a stallion and the other for a three-year old. It was merely the first of scores of records set at the track.

The track became part of Grand Circuit, a sort of NASCAR for harness racing. The meets were so popular that railroads ran special reduced rate excursion trains for big events. Thousands of spectators always filled the stands, rooting for their favorites.

But by far the most famous horse to speed around the track was the legendary Dan Patch. No horse had captured the public's imagination like the mahogany pacer foaled in Oxford, Indiana. He made several appearances in Terre Haute. Each was greatly anticipated by the fans who filled the stands. And woe to anyone who blocked the view. In those days of large hats, a female fan's chapeau was obstructing the sight lines to see the great horse. She ignored the pleas of fans behind and on either side of her to remove her hat. "Indeed I will not take off my hat….I did not fix my hair to remove it." She held fast despite rebukes from other female fans.

It was not just the shape of the track that enabled record-breaking performances. It was also meticulously maintained. In preparing the track for an 1897 meeting, for example, four hundred railroad cars of clay were brought in. The clay had to be harrowed, sprinkled and tamped down. Hordes of boys on their hands and knees were employed to pick out any stones or pebbles on the track.

Trainers and jockeys universally acclaimed the track as the finest in the country. No other track could boast such fine facilities for training horses. Spacious stables, good water, the bluegrass and its closeness to the railroad made it easy to load and unload horses and gear.

But the days of ten thousand people thronging the stands were soon over. Harness racing itself was in decline. A land syndicate bought the property to build upscale homes in the area. The last races were held in July 1910. Parts of track were torn down and moved to a half-mile oval course at the county fairgrounds. Sports returned to the site when Memorial Stadium opened in 1925. The stadium was then considered the finest minor-league baseball facility in the nation and played host to baseball, football and boxing matches. The stadium is still used by Indiana State University for football games.

But as the stadium opened, there were still those nostalgic harness racing fans who believed that they could still detect the aroma of hay, bluegrass and lathered horses wafting over the site.

WOODEN, WALKER AND WINNING

Even college coaching legends have to start somewhere. For John Wooden, the "Wizard of Westwood," who led his UCLA teams to ten NCAA championships, that place was Indiana State Teachers College in Terre Haute.

Wooden was a well-known entity in Indiana basketball circles. He starred on the 1927 Indiana high school champion Martinsville team and excelled as an All-American at Purdue. After coaching high school basketball in Dayton, Kentucky, and South Bend and serving in World War II, he accepted the head coaching position at ISTC in 1946. His contract paid him $3,500 to serve as athletic director, basketball coach and English instructor.

He succeeded his high school coach, Glen Curtis, at Indiana State. Curtis, who won four high school championships at Martinsville, was an Indiana State alum. Unlike his early years at UCLA, which had a distinctly undistinguished basketball tradition, Wooden inherited a well-established program at ISTC. Curtis had turned the Sycamores into a small college powerhouse. In his eight years in Terre Haute, Curtis's teams compiled a 122-45 record (.724 winning percentage) and made three postseason NAIB tournaments, finishing as runner-up in 1946.

Curtis had remained a mentor for Wooden and recommended him for the ISTC job. The new coach brought with him a style of basketball directly opposite that of his old high school coach. Curtis taught the traditional "defensive game" style of basketball that predominated that era. This plodding style emphasized defense and often agonizingly slow offense based on controlled dribbling to set up pre-designed plays. Teams would often "stall" the ball for minutes at a time looking for the ideal situation to run their plays. It was the age of the two-handed set shot. Winning scores over forty points were rarities.

But in the Midwest especially, a more up-tempo version of the game had been evolving since the 1930s. The new style emphasized speed and "fast break" basketball. It was the style Wooden (described as a whirling dervish on the court) had played at Purdue under legendary coach Ward "Piggy" Lambert. Lambert taught that passing, not dribbling, was the fastest way to get the ball up the court and did not allow the other team's defense time to set up to stop them.

So, in the fall of 1946, Wooden started putting together his first college team. Nearly 20 percent of the thousand-male student body tried out for the squad. That ridiculous number had to be whittled down, which cost precious time Wooden could have spent teaching basketball. It no doubt irritated the perfectionist coach. He mostly despaired of the local talent who stumbled through the try-outs. His final decision on who made the fifteen-man squad was a shock to many of the Terre Haute faithful. Local boys were few and far between. Three members from the previous team—Ed Lash, Jo DePugh and Bob Royer—made the squad, but so did eight players from South Bend and environs. Many members were World War II veterans, so it was an older team than usual. They were not callow eighteen-year-olds; most of them were in their twenties. Wooden pointed out that most of the holdovers were okay in Curtis's slowdown style but would not be able to handle the up-tempo game he wanted. Such explanations did little to muffle the outcry from disappointed fans.

But two newcomers would have a lasting impact, one on the history of college basketball and the other on Indiana State. Clarence Walker was a bright, thoughtful African American man from East Chicago. He was one of the "outsiders" recruited by Wooden. Though quick, he was never really

Wooden and his 1947–48 team. Clarence Walker is front and center. *Indiana State University Archives.*

more than a bench player. It would be games in which he never got to play that were to spur his legacy to basketball.

Indiana was a Jim Crow state. Segregation was a way of life in the Hoosier state. Clarence Walker had suffered under that system all his life. With Terre Haute being farther south than East Chicago, he wondered what he would find. Many Hoosiers had deep southern roots. Compared to East Chicago and Gary areas, Terre Haute had a miniscule black population, less than 5 percent. Terre Haute was not an easy place for Clarence Walker.

Walker kept a diary of his time at ISTC. It contained his thoughts about the school, life, his teammates and "J.C."—his shorthand for Jim Crow laws. He was a proud young man who felt himself the equal of anyone. While traveling with the team, he was refused service at restaurants, asked to go to "black" hotels or neighborhoods to find a bed and heard racial epithets cascading around him from fans. He hated Terre Haute but liked his teammates and greatly respected John Wooden.

After losing its first game of the 1946/47 season, Wooden's team began to take shape, and the local fans began to like the fast-paced style. The "Scrappin' Sycamores" came together and began winning. Wooden tempered the team by putting them in testing situations, like taking them into the challenging atmosphere of Madison Square Garden in New York. The Sycamores lost a tough game to St. John's–Brooklyn, but the experience made them tougher. The season was the coming-out party for a sophomore from Terre Haute named Duane Klueh. The tall, lean Klueh broke the school season scoring record.

At season's end, the Sycamores were once again invited to the National Association of Intercollegiate Basketball (NAIB) tournament in Kansas City. The invitation had little to do with the team's 17-9 record, however. As the runner-up in the 1946, ISTC received the automatic bid offered to teams that played in the tourney final of previous year.

The NAIB tournament was the first "national championship" in college basketball when it debuted in 1937, two years before the first NCAA tourney. The tournament was the brainchild of James Naismith, the "inventor" of basketball, and was designed for small colleges. The single-elimination tourney featured thirty-two of the best small college basketball teams in a weeklong orgy of hoops in Kansas City. Like other basketball tournaments, it did not allow black players to participate. That provision proved to be a vexing one for John Wooden.

Wooden was a man of integrity and committed to civil rights on a personal level. He often stood up against Jim Crow laws that affected Clarence Walker, including leaving restaurants that refused service to Walker. But he was reluctant to make a public stand. For instance, he did not take Walker when the team played at Madison Square Garden, presumably so he would not have to deal with the color barrier.

So, when the invitation to the 1947 tourney was announced, Wooden could have stood up against the tourney ban of "Negro" players. He could have said, "You take all of my team or none at all." Instead, after a bit of dithering, the college announced that it was not accepting the bid by disingenuously saying it was for academic reasons: it would take too much time away from the players' studies.

The 1947–48 squad benefited from a year of playing together, becoming fluid in the fast break game and toughening their defense. They started the season 10-1 and were known for their "scrappiness." They often came from behind, sparked by their tough defense and run-and-gun offense. They were led by Duane Klueh, who broke his own single-season scoring record. Once again they were invited to the NAIB tournament.

That invitation would have a different outcome from the year before, for both John Wooden and Clarence Walker. A bit of a myth has grown among many about John Wooden's direct role in breaking the color barrier in college basketball, sparked by Wooden's own later recollections. In fact, Wooden had decided to compete in the tourney and had left Walker's name off the tourney team list. The Sycamores and Wooden were fully prepared to enter the tourney without Clarence Walker.

Wooden was not the primary reason the NAIB broke with the precedent of banning "colored" ballplayers from competing. That honor belongs to three New York colleges that refused invitations to participate with the ban in place, as well as a member of the U.S. Olympic committee named Harry Henshel. Customarily, the winner of the NAIB tourney was automatically invited to the Olympic basketball team tryouts. Henshel and others threatened to withdraw the invitation unless the NAIB board abolished the ban. It worked. Not wanting to lose the prestige of the Olympic tryout, the NAIB lifted the ban.

When Clarence Walker entered the game against St. Francis (Pennsylvania) on that March 10 in Kansas City, he, like Jackie Robinson the summer before, broke another sport's color barrier. Walker played in all five tourney games, scoring eight points and committing eleven personal fouls. In that year's team photo in the ISTC yearbook, he is literally positioned front and center, holding the basketball.

The Sycamores sprinted through the first two games, overwhelming St. Francis and Brigham Young by thirty-two and fourteen points, respectively. Their Elite Eight game against San Jose State was a tighter affair, with ISTC winning, 59–52. Their semifinal game against Hamline College was a barn burner. The Sycamores led by twelve at halftime, but the Hamline squad dominated the second half. During the final seconds, ISTC trailed by two points, but Klueh was fouled while shooting and sank two free throws to send the game into overtime. Again Hamline was leading in the final seconds when Klueh threw up an underhand shot that went in. The Sycamores won, 66–65, and advanced to the championship game against highly favored Louisville. Their Cinderella slipper was smashed by the team from Kentucky, which defeated the Sycamores, 82–70. Klueh was named the tourney MVP.

Even before the tourney, Wooden was desperate to get out of Terre Haute. He had told friends and fellow coaches that he needed to find a new coaching job. Interestingly, it was an old childhood neighbor's decision that led Wooden to UCLA. The Wooden farm outside Monrovia, Indiana, butted against that of the McCracken family. John Wooden joined the McCracken boys in the makeshift court in their barn loft, using rolled-up socks as a basketball. Branch McCracken went on to become the legendary coach of the IU "Hurryin' Hoosiers," winning his first of two NCAA championship in 1940. In 1948, a West Coast school named UCLA was looking to boost its anemic basketball program. It looked to the Midwest, which had become a cradle of coaches. Their first choice was McCracken, who accepted the position. Having second thoughts, "Mac" asked Indiana to try to match the offer. He decided to stay at IU, but when he informed UCLA of his decision, he recommended for the job his old neighbor, the bright young coach at ISTC. Wooden happily left Terre Haute to forge his legend in L.A.

Clarence Walker stayed on, played basketball and was an honor student.

But winning basketball did not go away when Wooden departed. Led by senior Duane Klueh, who broke the all-time scoring record, the 1948–49 team continued winning and appearing in the NAIB championships under new coach John Longfellow. They finished fourth, but brighter days loomed.

In 1950, led by one of Wooden's South Bend recruits, Clemens "Lenny" Rzeszewski, the Sycamores finally won the coveted championship. Rzeszewski followed in the footsteps of Duane Klueh by being named the tourney MVP. Clarence Walker scored six of the team's final eight points in the championship game win over East Central (Ohio), 61–57.

Three Sycamores of the era—Bob Royer, John Hazen and Klueh—went on to play professional basketball in the newly formed Basketball of America Association, which became the NBA.

After two years in pro ball, Klueh successfully coached basketball at Fowler (IN) High School,before returning to his alma mater, where he coached basketball and tennis (Klueh was a champion tennis player). He coached Indiana State basketball for twelve years. His teams made three appearances in the NAIA (the new name of the NAIB) and two in the NCAA college division championships. He stepped down as basketball coach at the end of the 1967 season, after compiling a record of 182-122. He remained as a physical education instructor. Generations of Indiana State students knew him as the respected and beloved man simply known as "Coach."

PRIZEFIGHTING: "THUGS AND MURDEROUS TOUGHS"

Another popular Terre Haute sport was prizefighting. The problem was that it was illegal in Indiana.

Boxing, or prizefighting, had a long history, but it was considered barbaric by many. It was rightly felt that the boxing realm was populated by the less desirable elements in society—gamblers, thieves and ne'er-do-wells. Opponents pointed out that boxing matches were often held in saloons, gambling dens or brothels.

These views changed only slightly after the advent of the Marquess of Queensbury rules for prizefighting in 1867. Still, boxing had grown in popularity by the 1880s. Newspapers were filled with the exploits of John L. Sullivan and other prizefighters. Their bouts were often front-page news. This led many to call for the legalization—and regulation—of professional boxing matches. Doing so, noted an article in the *Terre Haute Express*, would help alleviate "what is objectionable in it." By that, it meant the unsavory characters most associated with the sport. The manly art, said one editorial, had passed into the hands of "thugs and murderous toughs."

The writer could have just as well have named Frank Trombley of Terre Haute as one of those thugs. The Canadian-born Trombley appeared in Terre Haute in the 1870s. He soon built his reputation as a bad man. Trombley was a well-known pimp, wife beater and thug. He was known as an inveterate gambler who too often resorted to violence as his solution of choice for any disagreement. He was an all-too-familiar face in the courts and jail. By 1880, he was married to Cora Lee, a Terre Haute madam, helping her run their brothel while organizing illegal gambling in the area. Lee later divorced Trombley, closed the brothel and moved to Chicago to escape his wrath.

That same year, he was charged with the attempted murder of Stephen Osborne. The unlucky Mr. Osborne had traveled from Sullivan, Indiana, with a friend to taste the nightlife of Terre Haute. While in the Tip Top saloon, Osborne drew the attention of Frank Trombley. Osborne said that Trombley approached him the back room and tried to kiss him. His advances rebuked, Trombley later confronted Osborne on the street and attempted to kill him. After several mistrials, Trombley, called a "wretch and Terror," was sentenced to prison.

He was not long out of prison when he was again in trouble. Trombley, who then lived on a houseboat on the Wabash, was apparently hosting the wife of a Mr. Cooper. Finding his wife absent from their home, Cooper made his way to the riverbank with ideas of retrieving his errant spouse. He was met by a load of buckshot with his name on it. Trombley later claimed that the unfortunate Mr. Cooper had blundered into his gunsight as he was attempting to shoot a pigeon and it was all a terrible mistake.

After a failed suicide attempt using morphine in 1885, Trombley, who fancied himself a pugilist, became increasingly involved in boxing. In 1886, he announced that he would take on all comers in a prizefight, using hard gloves. His hard-glove challenge was taken up by Terre Haute policeman Tom Connelly. They agreed to fight in a twenty-four-foot ring on a boat in the Wabash (such illegal bouts were often held in the middle of rivers due to uncertainty about which entity had jurisdiction). Eventually, the boat was floated to a location farther below Terre Haute. It was attended by a barge holding spectators and a bar stocked with liquor and twenty kegs of beer. Who won the bout was a point of contention afterward.

Trombley continued to be the center of illicit boxing in the area. In 1888, he spread word that he was staging a bout between two "colored pugilists," Black Star Johnson and "Thompson, the iron jawed man" in Macksville (now West Terre Haute). Bouts between African American fighters were prevalent during the era. To the many who viewed African Americans as less than human, it was akin to cockfighting or bear-baiting.

Spectators, who paid $2.50 (equivalent to $60.00 today), were not told the location of the fight until early evening to prevent law enforcement from shutting down the bout. Finally, word spread that the bout would take place in a barn along the Vandalia Railroad west of Macksville. Terre Haute's sporting fraternity headed west. The bout began at 10:30 p.m. on April 5, 1888, after it was announced it would be fought under Marquess of Queensbury rules using four-ounce gloves (modern gloves are ten to twelve ounces). It was forecast as a grudge match between Johnson, the "scientific fighter," and Thompson's raw power.

The bout was barely a minute old when Johnson's powerful right hand collided with Thompson's supposed iron jaw. Thompson hit the floor. Thompson rose and continued the fight, which seemed even until the fifth round. Thompson's powerful blow sent Johnson staggering, sprawling to the floor. Johnson lay on the floor in a fetal position. He raised his hand saying that he "had enough." He finally struggled to his feet. Evidently, Thompson did not agree that enough was enough and proceeded to pummel the slumping Johnson until he knocked him out of the ring. There the beaten man crumpled at the feet of the sweating, screaming, fervid fans. He made twenty-five dollars for his beating.

Trombley continued to promote illegal fights, being indicted for them and paying his fines with his profits. Prizefighting in Indiana was not legalized until the 1920s.

Disasters

Sandford's Month of Terror

The scheduled train from Indianapolis to Mattoon pulled out of the Terre Haute Big Four Depot around 8:30 p.m. on Saturday, January 19, 1907. It was an "accommodation" train, which meant it stopped at each station along the route. Pulling three passenger coaches and one baggage car, the engine chugged across the trestle bridge over the Wabash River. A message had been sent earlier, and a freight train was pulled over onto a siding at tiny Sandford, Indiana. Passenger trains were usually given the right-of-way on the tracks over freight carriers. There were more than sixty passengers scattered among the three cars on the accommodation train, among them Bud Wolf, his wife and their two young daughters. They lived in Sandford and looked forward to getting home. At about 8:50 p.m., the train slowed and pulled into the tiny Sandford station. It would go no farther.

Before the departing passengers could stand, stretch and make their way to the exits, there was an ear-shattering, ground-shaking explosion. The tremors were felt more than thirty miles away. Many people thought an earthquake was shaking their world. Those closer to Sandford saw a fireball shoot heavenward in the dark sky. Soon an orange glow, almost like a fiery cloud, rose up from Sandford, making the dark night light again. Otherworldly screams shared the air with the crackling of flames and the hiss of steel and iron bending in the forge-like heat.

The thirty-four-car freight train was carrying one hundred kegs marked "Black Powder." They exploded, each keg a small bomb that united with the others to destroy everything in its path with a determined vengeance. After their initial shock abated somewhat, the people looked toward the scene. It was not an earthquake or a fiery ball from the heavens that shook them to their core, they realized, but a train that had exploded. Then, as a newspaper later reported, terror reigned in Sandford.

Senses regained, many ran to the station in a pouring rain to see if they could help. What they saw was a Dante-esque level of hell that they hoped never to encounter. The passenger train engine was blown a hundred yards away. One thousand yards of track were a smoldering spaghetti of steel. All the cars of the passenger train were blown off the track. Freight cars all but disappeared as though atomized by the explosion. There was only a deep crater where the car holding the black powder once stood. The scene was a giant "funeral pyre."

Rescuers from the village were greeted by the cries of the injured. They could see people trapped in the mangled cars, but when they tried to reach the stricken, they were driven back by the intense heat. Stunned rescuers could only watch as victims burned alive. Bodies were everywhere. Finally,

Damaged tracks at Sanford. *Vigo County Historical Society.*

as the heat subsided, they were able to pull some survivors from the steaming wreckage. Some tied wet handkerchiefs across their faces in a vain attempt to ward off the smell of burnt flesh.

Two local doctors, J.T. Brown and C.E. Ray, performed triage, treating the most seriously wounded at the scene, sending the walking wounded to their offices and those beyond their powers to the temporary morgue set up in the station. Dr. Brown worked without rest for more than twenty-four hours, only taking a break when an additional twenty doctors arrived by Sunday evening. Residents opened their houses as makeshift emergency rooms. Housewives instantly became nurses, tending to the injured. Later, a train arrived from Paris, Illinois, loaded with doctors and railroad personnel. The injured were loaded onto the train and taken to the hospital in Paris.

The explosion cut the telegraph lines. For nearly an hour, the people of Sandford were the only first responders. A man volunteered to walk ten miles along the same tracks the passenger train had traveled to Terre Haute to seek assistance.

Rescuers continued their grisly tasks throughout the sodden night. With flickering lanterns, they found bodies or parts of bodies strewn across the area. Looking up, they spied the body of a young man or

Sandford destruction. *Vigo County Historical Society*.

boy dangling nearly one hundred feet above them on a tree hundreds of yards from the wreckage. They tripped over bits of luggage, shoes, clothing and the occasional hand or arm that had been almost surgically severed from bodies.

The wreckage site was no less startling or sickening with the coming of the day. The cloying, stifling smell of charred flesh hung like a cloud over everything. Charles Piker was a Big Four section hand who had seen more than his share of train wrecks, but nothing in his past prepared him for Sandford. The destruction and lives lost made him weep. "It is the worst experience of my life," he later told a reporter. "I shall never forget that night. It seems God chose the worst night possible for the accident. It was cold and windy and dark. It is tragic to think of the suffering."

Sunday and Monday were spent trying to identify the dead. Two days after the explosion, there were still five bodies that could not be identified. One was listed only as "Aged Woman, burnt beyond recognition." Four bodies were found in the woods. They were believed to be the bodies of a fireman on the passenger train and Mrs. Wolf and her two daughters. Their remains were taken to the morgue to be united with their husband and father.

Railroad authorities tried to piece together what happened. A Sandford man said he thought he saw a drunk or tramp fire a shot into the freight car. No one else recalled seeing this mystery man. Some posited that lightning may have set off the explosion, but no one saw a bolt strike the train. Big Four authorities decided that the most likely cause was that the freight train stood above an oil pipeline and gases emitted by the line were ignited by a spark from the wheels of the passenger train.

Looking at the incredible damage, some speculated that the kegs did not contain black powder as marked but held dynamite instead. It was well known that some shippers purposely mislabeled dynamite shipments as gunpowder because the shipping rate was 80 percent cheaper than for explosives like dynamite. Around 1:00 a.m., a "wrecking train" arrived to begin the work clearing the wreckage. Thomas Gorman was the foreman in charge of a ten-man crew. They worked continually, but it still took them until Tuesday to clean up the site. Gorman had been in the wrecking business for thirty-eight years and had seldom seen so much devastation from a train wreck.

Five days after the explosion, the *Terre Haute Tribune* received an anonymous letter purporting to know the truth about the explosion's cause. The editor decided to publish this odd missive with the warning that it "may be true… or the imaginings of a distempered brain." The typewritten letter was rather florid but did reveal that the author was an educated man. He was fascinated

Newspaper drawing of Sandford's horrors. *Vigo County Historical Society.*

by the various theories about the explosion's causes, but "no human being besides myself suspect the truth."

He spun a tale of two men and one woman who attended school together. Using false names, he told the stories of Minnie Winters, Jack Hastings and (the appropriately named) William Black. He described Minnie as a young girl of "remarkable attractiveness, of personal grace and splendid character." Jack Hastings was the ordinary plodding type of young man, but one of the "greatest integrity and most unimpeachable character." William Black, however, was the quintessential bad boy. He was intelligent, quick-witted and the most "daring even desperate of young men."

The three were friends during their school days. Minnie and William were the brightest in their class, usually sharing academic honors. Many who knew them believed they would eventually marry. But William had his dark side, even as a youth. "No orchard was robbed that William Black did not plan" and "no small deviltry took place" that Black did not instigate. The deviltries would become crimes as he grew older.

Black was later suspected as the murderer of an itinerant peddler, but nothing could be proven. Still, the suspicion was so strong that Black felt that "Terre Haute was not conducive to his health, and he left for parts unknown even to his parents." He returned five years later, with the rumor that he had taken part in a massacre of Mexicans in Arizona trailing behind him. His first question of the old folks was about what happened to Minnie. He was shocked to hear that she had married Jack Hastings and moved away. He tracked the couple down and visited them at their new home. The sight of his true love married to a man he considered much his inferior sent him back on the road.

In the following years, Black "travelled constantly and begged and stole insistently" and "degenerated into the commonest kind of crook." He rode the rails and once had to fight for his life after a disagreement with his partners over dividing the spoils of their recent robbery of a grocery store. Once again he returned to Terre Haute, carrying with him his delusions about what his life would have been with Minnie at his side. He went to visit her and declared his true love, but she sent him away. More and more the dreams of what might have been tortured him. He secured a bomb from someone and went once again to see Minnie. Hearing that she was gone but would return soon, he went to Sandford to meet the train. Hatred gripped his hand as he lit the bomb and pushed it under the powder car.

Thus ends the tale of Minnie, Jack and William Black. Was it "the truth" about the disaster, as the author proclaimed? Almost certainly not. Was it just a hoax? Almost certainly yes. But who was the teller of this tale? Was it "William Black" himself? Was it the work of the Big Four railroad in an attempt to absolve itself of any blame so as not to pay damages? History sometimes keep it secrets, no matter how many try to uncover them.

The village of Sandford was still coming to terms with the wreck after a month. Many were having a hard time dealing with what they had witnessed, and many were still repairing damage to their own homes from the explosion. They were not ready for the terror that struck them on the night of February 21.

Those who came out saw that the Methodist church had been blown up. Oddly, they just retreated to their homes, not bothering to report it. Some saw it as another "terrorist" act, possibly the work of criminals in the area. They could not ignore it for long. Several hours later, there were two more explosions. This time, two general stores were dynamited. Afterward, the bombings were reported to authorities in Terre Haute. By morning, police and sheriffs had begun an investigation. The thoughts of many in Sandford immediately turned to a man they felt was capable of such a crime—or any crime, for that matter.

Sandford was unincorporated village, which meant it did not have a law enforcement officer. Oddly, it also straddled two states. Being on the state line, the eastern part of the village was in Indiana, while its western edge was in Illinois. Both reasons attracted a lawless element. If someone committed a crime in one section of town, they only had to walk a few feet to be in the other jurisdiction. Among the lawless was a man named Henry F. McDonald.

Born in Redmon, Illinois, in 1874, McDonald had been a fireman, farmer and miner. He was also known as a man with a hair-trigger temper who loved to use his fists (he had been a boxer) to settle scores. By 1906, he was in the liquor business as the owner of a "quart shop" in Sandford. Quart shops were basically liquor wholesalers. They could only sell in bulk. In McDonald's case, this meant the minimum amount he could sell was five gallons. His business was a source of great tension. Sandford was in Fayette Township, which was officially "dry." Local ministers and storekeepers were always pushing to have his operation shut down. They reported that he was operating a "blind tiger," a joint selling liquor illegally. That did not go down well with McDonald, a man with an outsized sense of grievance who spewed threats at anyone he felt had crossed him.

Terre Haute chief of detectives Bill Dwyer and his men were on scene the morning after the bombings. Significantly, one other man was helping in the investigation, a Big Four railroad detective named Brim. The people of Sandford were not anxious to talk with the detectives, fearing retribution from the perpetrators. Several men, worried about their family's safety, sent their wives and children to Terre Haute and Paris until they felt it was safe for them to return.

Meanwhile, police raided McDonald's shop and seized twenty-five cases of bottled beer, which was legally considered evidence that he was operating a blind tiger. They arrested McDonald and his bartender, Bill Scanlon, on minor charges of drunkenness. Adding to McDonald's sense of grievance, they took the beer to Terre Haute using his own team and wagon. The pair quickly made bail, and Scanlon immediately went to a local brewery and bought more cases of beer. Being prime suspects, they were under police surveillance.

James Reece, whose store was destroyed, said he could identify a suspect. He saw a tall man running from his store, and a few seconds later the dynamite exploded. Henry McDonald was listed as "tall" on his World War I draft registration form. Another man said that he knew who did it but would not testify in court out of fear. It was pointed out that the placement of the dynamite indicated that the bombers did not want anyone to be killed—only that the properties be destroyed as a warning.

It did not take long for many to connect the bombings with the railroad disaster. Big Four railroad officials pushed that scenario relentlessly. If they could prove a connection, it meant they could not be found culpable and thus not liable for damage suits.

Feeling that there was strong circumstantial evidence against McDonald and Scanlon, the prosecutor ordered the pair arrested on February 27. They were formally indicted on March 4. McDonald remained in jail until August, when he finally made bail. McDonald returned to Sandford saying that he held no grudge, seemingly a first in his querulous life. The case finally came to trial in January 1908. It was accompanied by the usual McDonaldian vows of revenge if convicted. After listening to the arguments, the members of the jury were sent off to return with a verdict. This they could not do. After twenty-nine hours and four votes, they reported that they could not agree on a verdict. The judge declared a mistrial. Later, it was leaked that the jury voted eleven to one to convict, but a stubborn holdout refused to find him guilty.

But the prosecutor, John Cooper, was not about to let the crime go unpunished. A re-trial was scheduled for April. Angered that his ordeal was not over, McDonald publicly announced that all hell would be loosened if he were convicted. The trial took place. This time, all twelve jurors agreed that he was guilty of the bombings.

McDonald kept his promise.

Moments after the reading of the verdict, McDonald reached into his pocket and pulled out a wicked-looking .38 Colt revolver. Before anyone had time to ponder why a defendant was allowed to bring a firearm into court, McDonald pulled the trigger. He missed his primary target, as Prosecutor Cooper managed to dive under the table and avoid the bullet ticketed for him. McDonald got off at least one more shot. This time, the bullet was unerring, and Chief of Detectives Dwyer, the man McDonald felt was his primary persecutor, fell dead. The next shots came from other policemen in the court. At least three shots dropped McDonald, but he was still alive.

McDonald was taken to St. Anthony Hospital and put on suicide watch. That precaution seemed irrelevant during the first four days. Twice it seemed that McDonald was very near death, but he gradually got better. He continually proclaimed himself innocent of the bombings. He remained in the hospital for nearly six weeks before doctors declared him fit to stand trial. McDonald was immediately transferred from the hospital to a well-guarded jail cell.

Although he continued to sing his song of innocence, McDonald freely admitted that the murder of Dwyer was premeditated. He believed Dwyer was actually working with the Big Four railroad to set him up as the patsy for both the bombings and wrecking the trains. "Someone had to drop," he said, if he was found guilty. He vowed that he had decided to "take someone with me." His plan was to kill Cooper and Dwyer and then turn the gun on himself.

His murder trial ended in March 1908. His insanity defense did not help him. He was convicted of murdering Dwyer and attempted murder of Cooper. Normally, it would have been a textbook case for capital punishment, but the judge was uncommonly lenient. He sentenced McDonald to only two to twenty-one years in state prison. This puzzled some, but it seemed that many people in Terre Haute felt he had indeed been railroaded by the Big Four and was innocent of the bombings. Later, when he came up for parole, eight thousand people signed a petition asking it be granted. Just as it seemed he would be freed, Indiana governor Frank Hanly stepped in to quash it.

McDonald was paroled in 1918 after serving ten years. One of the first people he called on was Cooper. He apologized for trying to kill him and promised that he would lead an unblemished life from then on. Cooper even arranged for a lucrative job for him. McDonald settled in Fontanet northeast of Terre Haute, where his parents lived. It was hard for him to lead an unblemished life as he had promised.

Henry McDonald was killed in 1925 when he struggled with Vigo County sheriff Ray Foncannon, who was trying to disarm him. The sheriff had been investigating a call from Fontanet that said McDonald was running a blind tiger and terrorizing the neighborhood. That story can be found in the book *Wicked Terre Haute*.

The Home Packing Explosion

Henry Akers was blown so high that he remembered pleading, "Please, God, let me live" five times before he landed.

The employees of the Home Packing Company shuffled into work on January 2, 1963, after a four-day holiday break. Home Packing covered two blocks on North First Street along the Wabash River. Founded in 1907, the company was an institution in Terre Haute known for its Dependable brand of pork products.

Just after 7:00 a.m., the two-story building shuddered and then began collapsing. First its walls began crumbling, and the roof quite literally fell in, as if the building were a house of cards tumbling down. Debris cascaded down on the workers. Those in the slaughtering, cutting and curing rooms found themselves trapped in a whirlwind of meat, steel, iron, brick and plaster. The freezer unit on the first floor plummeted into the basement.

Jim Walker, a meat cutter, was on the second floor when he heard an explosion that sounded like someone slamming a big door closed. Bob Boerner felt the floor beneath his feet cave in, followed by the ceiling falling down on him. "Everything went black," he said. Stunned, he managed come to his senses and slowly crawl along the floor until he saw daylight. Mitchell Kernstein felt as if a "whirlwind grabbed hold of me and shook my teeth." Meat cutter Richard Brown had just stepped outside the building when the explosion blew him twenty feet away into the parking lot. Ed Bland was also outside the southern side of the building. When he felt the explosion, he started running to see what happened as bricks began falling like rain around him. He could hear the shouts of his friends calling out for help, but there was nothing he could do. "The sides of the building gave in," he recounted, "then all of it seemed to blow up." The explosion's force was so fierce that it blew a freight car off the siding outside the building.

Response to the disaster was quick. Soon there were ten fire apparatus stationed around the rubble. Firemen wearing gas masks to protect them from ammonia fumes began to shift debris looking for victims. Word spread quickly, and a legion of rescuers rushed to the site. Trucking companies volunteered their trucks and other equipment to help clear the debris. City and county workers dropped what they were doing to help in any way they could. The Red Cross set up canteens and brought in relief and medical supplies. National Guard and Civil Defense crews were called in.

One of the most valuable units was the local mine rescue emergency team. It was used to working in such disasters. The collapse of the building was very similar to the conditions these men encountered in mine explosions or accidents. They were key in knowing when to slow down and not just rush into an area. They shored up teetering walls to ensure they did not collapse on rescuers and make things worse.

Dazed workers crawled out or were pulled from the debris by grasping hands. They were treated on site, and those needing more care were transported to the two local hospitals. An emergency first-aid facility was set up at the County Highway garage a few blocks south. Later, it would also serve as a temporary morgue. One man still trapped in rubble up to his shoulders was given a shot of painkiller by one of the doctors who hurried to the scene. They told him it would be a long time before they could extricate him.

Collapse of Home Packing walls. *Vigo County Historical Society*.

Piece by piece, debris was snatched by hundreds of fevered hands to clear a path for rescuers. Sometimes victims were seen long before a rescue could be attempted. Don Scott, brother of Home Packing's president, could be seen sitting at his desk but was too covered by debris to be rescued immediately. When they finally reached him, they confirmed only that he was dead.

Rescued workers explained the layout of the plant and where others were still trapped. James Tidd knew there were still men in one of the coolers. He and others pounded on the door to see if there were any survivors. They tried to push open the heavy door, but a part of the ceiling had caved in behind it. They had no choice but to try to get out before they became trapped themselves.

Worried family members seeking news of their loved ones joined the throng of onlookers. Some were directed to the hospitals. There among gurneys neatly lining the walls, they sought out familiar faces. The ammonia fumes were so strong on the bodies of those hospitalized that nurses and doctors had to don gas masks provided by the local Air Guard unit. In schools around the area, students whose fathers worked at the plant were quietly pulled from class, told of the explosion and sent home to be with their families.

All through the day and into the long, cold night, rescuers pulled and tugged and searched. Heavy equipment like drag lines and bulldozers were called in to speed debris removal. The responders knew that with each passing minute, the chances of finding survivors grew less likely. What they found were lifeless bodies. Some had been crushed by debris, some succumbed to ammonia fumes and some were scalded by boiling steam released by pipe ruptures.

While the grim work continued, the experts searched for the cause of the explosion. Initially, some thought that a boiler exploded or that an ammonia gas leak had triggered the disaster. Those were quickly ruled out, as the boiler had not exploded and an expert noted that ammonia was not capable of igniting in that manner.

It did not take them long to focus on a natural gas explosion. Terre Haute fire chief Norman Fesler noted that it looked like "everything blew from the bottom up and caved in." One expert said the site had "all characteristics of a natural gas explosion." An investigator from the Indiana Fire Marshal's Office seized a thirty-seven-inch section of gas pipe where a leak had been discovered. He sent it to the Indiana State Police lab. Local authorities immediately demanded that it be returned. Within days, it was determined that the cause was indeed natural gas. A leaking main outside the plant allowed gas to seep through the ground and accumulate under the building during the holiday shutdown. All it took was a spark.

The cleanup begins. *Vigo County Historical Society.*

Note the railroad car blown off tracks by the explosion. *Vigo County Historical Society.*

The Terre Haute community rallied around. A relief fund for the families was set up within twenty-four hours. Donations flowed in. Home Packing president Robert Scott announced that employees would receive emergency checks for a full week's pay. Later, he added full vacation pay for the year.

The first of sixty-four civil suits against the Terre Haute Gas Corporation was filed four days after the explosion. It charged that the company failed to properly maintain the pipes, leading to the leaks. Interestingly, it also sought a restraining order preventing the "secreting of evidence" by the company. Later, Home Packing also sued the gas company. The families' suits were settled in 1964—$9 million was paid to survivors. The Home Packing suit against the gas company dragged on until 1966, when an out-of-court settlement (reportedly for $5 million) was reached.

More than twenty-eight hours after the disaster, the last body was pulled from the rubble. The Home Packing disaster caused the death of seventeen men, injured more than fifty and irrevocably altered the lives of many, many more.

There was some talk of rebuilding the company, but it was not to be. Besides haunted memories, all that remains of the Home Packing Company is a weathered cornerstone on the site.

Arts and Letters

The Miniaturist and the Diva

For two talented young women, Terre Haute simply did not provide a big enough stage on which to play out their lives. One strode the national stage, while the other became an international sensation.

Amalia Kussner's life resembled a fairytale—or perhaps a bad made-for-TV movie. She found fame, married into riches, traveled the world and consorted with royalty.

Amalia Kussner, born in 1862, was from a talented family. Her father was a musician and well-regarded composer of German instrumental music and *Lieder*, and her sister an accomplished vocalist. The Kussner family moved to Terre Haute during the Civil War, with her father opening a music shop.

She displayed artistic talent early that eventually resulted in the art form that would make her famous: painting miniature portraits and landscapes. She would specialize in miniatures painted on ivory but also was an accomplished fore-edge painter, in which scenes were painted on the edges of book pages. It was said that when she ran out of ivory discs she would seek out damaged piano keys her father discarded.

She attended school in Terre Haute and received an award for an outstanding essay when she graduated from Terre Haute High School in 1881. Her essay, titled "Money Lost, Nothing Lost; Honor Lost, Much Lost; Courage Lost, All Lost," was typical of the high-minded sentiments of the day. She then studied art at St. Mary-of-the-Woods College.

Amalia Kussner Coudert.
Vigo County Historical Society.

In 1883, Kussner went to New York to attend Madame Da Silva's very fashionable boarding school. She also received more formal training at New York's Art Institute League. Returning to Terre Haute in 1885, she opened an art studio, concentrating on decorative and landscape painting. She received plaudits for her decorative paintings on china and began what would become her specialty: the painting of miniature portraits of prominent people on ivory discs.

Realizing that Terre Haute had given her all it could offer, the thirty-year-old Kussner moved to New York in 1892. She was reportedly invited east by an old classmate named Alice Fischer, who was making a name for herself there as an actress. Accompanied by her mother, Kussner opened a studio in a fashionable area of the city. A letter of introduction to Louisine Havemeyer set the stage for her career. Havemeyer was incredibly influential in the art world. She was an early patron of impressionists like Claude Monet, and she and her husband built up the finest private art collection in the nation. When Kussner exhibited her work at a fashionable Fifth Avenue gallery in 1894, an article in the *New York Sun* praised her work. The publicity brought her to the attention of fashionable New York society types. Her portrait of Caroline Astor, doyenne of the trendy 400, made her the most sought-after artist in the city.

By 1895, Kussner was the darling of the New York art world. A fulsome article in *Harper's Bazaar* credited her with revitalizing the art of miniatures and calling her "the high priestess of the daintiest of arts." Kussner was making $400 to $600 per painting. She traveled to Europe in 1895 and immediately was welcomed into the world of royalty and the aristocracy. She was invited to Blenheim Palace in 1896. There she did a miniature of the Duchess of Marlborough, Winston Churchill's grandmother. Her clients were a veritable list of the high-born, posh and wealthy women of Victorian England: Lady Colebrooke, Lady Dudley and Lady Sturt, among others. The influential British publication *The Sketch* published a glowing article about the young American artist. Part of Kussner's allure was her supposed youth, but she had long ago begun pruning years off her age. Even though she was actually thirty-four years old in 1896, she only admitted to being twenty-three or twenty-four.

Kussner began traveling the world as a tourist and working artist. She went to South Africa in 1899 to paint diamond king and empire-maker Cecil Rhodes. Disembarking in Capetown, she traveled to Kimberly to meet Rhodes. Unfortunately, she arrived just before the Boers besieged the town during the Boer War. She was trapped there when the Boer bombardment terrorized the city. The city was placed on starvation rations. Newspapers breathlessly ran stories that Kussner could be killed by a bomb at any moment or could starve. They did not know that she was a guest in Rhodes's bombproof underground shelter or that his guests most assuredly did not starve. She had trouble getting the peripatetic Rhodes to sit still. She did manage to escape as the siege was lifted and made it back to London in January 1900. She later finished the Rhodes portrait from memory.

The year 1900 was a momentous one for Kussner. Earlier, she had met her future husband while traveling in France. Colonel Charles DuPont Coudert was a wealthy international lawyer who had served in the army in

Left: Amalia Kussner Coudert, Annie Wainwright Scott Strong, circa 1894, watercolor on ivory. *Collection of Swope Art Museum, Terre Haute; Gift of Lewis Hoyer Rabbage in honor of Frances Hughes, 1995.13.*

Right: Amalia Kussner Coudert, Matilda Thora Wainwright Scott Strong, circa 1894–95, watercolor on ivory. *Collection of Swope Art Museum, Terre Haute; Gift of Lewis Hoyer Rabbage in honor of Frances Hughes, 1995.*

the Philippines. The couple were married on July 3, 1900, in a rather hasty ceremony (they were not supposed to marry until the fall) at St. Patrick's Cathedral in New York. Being Protestant, Kussner had to receive special dispensation to be married there. Oddly, only their mothers attended the wedding. Whether the twenty-eight-year-old groom knew that his wife was actually ten years older than him is unknown.

Less than a year later, Amalia Coudert was the defendant in a highly secretive court case. A woman named Blanche Lincoln (probably a false name to ensure anonymity) sued Coudert for $125,000, nearly $4 million in modern valuation. By agreement, none of the attorneys for either side appeared in court, which meant Lincoln won the case by default. Why the secrecy? The *New York Times* called it a "mystery four feet thick." Perhaps "Miss Lincoln" was a former fiancée of Captain Coudert and sued Amalia for alienation of affections. But that is mere conjecture.

Coudert's parents gave them the family mansion in New York as a wedding gift. But it appears they were seldom there. They spent much of their time in England and Europe. They were given an audience with Pope Pius X in 1904. He presented them with a portrait of himself signed "to the little married couple, Amalia and DuPont Coudert." The couple moved to a castle in Surrey, England, in 1914. By that time, Amalia had stopped painting, at least for the public.

The little girl from Terre Haute, Indiana, died in the playground of the rich, Montreaux, Switzerland, in 1932.

VALESKA SURATT WAS AN enigmatic women. As Vigo County Historian Mike McCormick noted, it was difficult to know if she was a "[c]oquette, vamp, humanitarian or religious zealot."

Born in 1882, Valeska was the daughter of blacksmith Ralph Surratt and his wife, Anna. She recalled growing up "poor, quite poor." She hated wearing hand-me-down clothes, which may explain her later penchant for exotic costumes and dresses. Valeska was a free spirit who was bored by school. After she became a famous actress, locals recalled that she was always "star struck," although she later denied that was the case. Terre Haute had a lively stage scene during her youth, with many theaters that hosted traveling entertainers and numerous amateur productions, but she did not take part in any of them.

However, fashion did interest her, particularly hats. She told of making hats for her dolls as a child and doing the hair of her playmates. She and sister Leah worked at a hat shop at the Deming Hotel in downtown Terre Haute, where Valeska designed hats for customers. At seventeen, she moved to Indianapolis to work in the millinery department at Block's Department Store. Four years later, she was in Chicago, reportedly to study voice and acting. From there, her story takes on shades of Hollywood mythmaking. In a story almost surely the work of the perfervid imagination of a press agent, it was said that a Russian grand duke was so struck by her beauty that he wrote her a check for $1,000 on the spot to help finance her dreams, and she never saw him again. A later invention said that she was the only performer ever asked to give a command performance for a Russian tsar (also the shah of Iran). It was there, it was said, where the grand duke gave her the check, although the next day he was blown to bits by an anarchist's bomb.

A more likely but probably still exaggerated story was later attested to by her sister, Leah. Her sister is said to have purchased a $0.25 ticket for a Honduran lottery scheme. To her great luck, Leah won $1,000. If so, she was lucky. The Honduran lottery was considered a "colossal scheme of larceny" known for not paying out prizes to winners. Upon hearing of her sister's good fortune, Valeska immediately returned to Terre Haute and took the money to finance her search for stardom in New York.

The young woman who stepped off the train in New York City in 1903 or 1904 (some sources give the date as 1905, but she married her vaudeville partner Billy Gould in 1904) was certainly striking looking. At five-foot-eight, she was always described as statuesque. One writer described her as "Juno-esque" after the mythic Roman goddess. She changed the spelling of her name by dropping an *r*. Whether this was a mere whim or due to the lingering memory of the Surratt family of Baltimore being key members of the Lincoln assassination plot is unknown. What she didn't possess was an overabundance of talent. Walter Winchell, king of gossip columnists, said, "She acts not, and neither does she sing—she has a body rather than a figure." He likened her to a seductive, smiling python. An admirer admitted that she did not have natural talent, except for her throaty, vibrant voice that he recalled with great pleasure long after. Suratt admitted that others were better actors, dancers and singers. "It's my personality that wins for me. I'm no singer. Heaps of people can beat me dancing. Precious few of them, though, get the salary I do. Why? Because I'm me."

What she had was *presence*. Men and women took notice of Valeska Suratt and her style sense. She was the "first to feature dead, pale makeup, blood red lips, her hair swept straight back." People commented on her luxuriant "Titian hair." Even her passport description was a catalogue of beauty, noting her high forehead, straight nose, full mouth, dimpled chin, fair complexion and oval chin. She later wrote a widely syndicated column devoted to beauty tips and had her own line of makeup.

But most of all, it was her clothes. Suratt admitted that the talent many saw in her was "the clothes I wore and the way I wore them." "No other woman," a columnist said, "had her flair for the bizarre in clothing." She was the first to "drape herself in clinging velvet gowns." She scandalized many with slit skirts cut high on her thigh. Perhaps her most famous look was dresses that plunged down to her waist in the back. A writer cleverly noted she was "a beauty whose back was as celebrated as Chaplin's walk."

She first tried to be a chorus girl, but despite her long legs and presence, she was not an accomplished dancer. Her big break supposedly came in a "Lana Turner in Schwab's Drugstore" moment. Supposedly, she traveled to London to try the stage there. One evening, she was walking down the staircase in an elegant dress at the Savoy Hotel in 1905 when she was spotted by a producer, who immediately announced that she was just the one to play a Gibson Girl in his new play and whisked her on a boat back to New York. It seems like another press agent concoction. There are no extant records of her on passenger lists to Europe at the time, and she did not apply for her passport until 1917.

Instead, she was likely performing her vaudeville act with her husband, Billy Gould, and was spotted there. At any rate, she was cast as the Gibson Girl in *A Belle of Mayfair*. The rather frivolous play was a hit and did indeed make Valeska Suratt a star. The next decade saw her appear in numerous Broadway plays and vaudeville shows and tour with her own theater company. She was one of the highest-paid entertainers in the world.

Along the way, she became known for pushing the boundaries of propriety on stage. Her repertoire was replete with bawdy songs filled with sexual innuendo. Her costumes were also noticed by the police, and many thought her obscene. It all came to a head when she appeared in *The Girl with the Whooping Cough*.

The "plot" of this thin 1910 tale has Suratt playing Regina, a young girl who gives the whooping cough to the many men she kisses. The denouement of the play finds Regina in divorce court, at which she breaks into one of the bawdy dances from her vaudeville routine. The playbill shows Suratt in a fur-trimmed gown draped over only one shoulder. The other shoulder is bare down to the side of her breast. The obvious intention was to titillate theatergoers into thinking that any movement might result in a brief glimpse of her breast.

Like Queen Victoria, the mayor of New York was not amused. After hearing the show's tryout in Trenton had raised eyebrows, Mayor William Gaynor asked to see the script. He approved it, but when the show opened, he realized that he had been given an expurgated script and things had been added back into the production. He tasked the police commissioner with suppressing the show and announced that the theater's license would not be renewed unless it canceled the show. The show's producers got an injunction to keep the show running. However, the ruling stated that the city did not have to renew the lease. Without a theater, the production was closed down and taken on the road. Reviews calling it vulgar, stupid and "disgusting in its futile efforts to be risqué" ensured that it played to packed houses on the road.

The next year, Suratt was enveloped in a personal scandal. She divorced her husband and vaudeville partner, Billy Gould, in 1910. Within months, she married Fletcher Norton, a California actor who appeared in several of her

Poster for Valeska Suratt, the "Bell of the Boulevard." *Author's collection.*

shows. But by December 1911, a court referee filed a report with the New York Supreme Court recommending that Fletcher Norton be given a divorce decree. The report said it was to dissolve a marriage that "offended the sense of decency." It seems that Suratt only married Norton because she was angry at her live-in lover, Richard Mackey, and did it to spite him. She regretted it immediately. Evidently, the couple did not sign the final papers. Although they don't appear to have lived together, each listed the other as spouse until Norton's death in California in 1941.

The scandal certainly didn't hinder Suratt's career. She continued to star in plays and vaudeville and remained immensely popular. She returned to Terre Haute several times and staged her shows in local theaters. Her next big career move was one that would stamp her as a sex symbol for a worldwide audience.

In 1914, she signed a contract with Laskey Players to appear in movies. But before making a film for Laskey, she jumped to Fox Films for more money. She made eleven films for Fox between 1915 and 1917, none of which survive. In films like *The Siren*, *Wife Number Two* and *Rich Man's Plaything*, she was invariably cast as the vamp. The films played around the globe, and some believed she rivaled the renowned Theda Bara as the personification of the type.

Suratt returned to the stage after her Hollywood years but evidently longed for more. Her last performance was in 1924. Her remaining years were a search for something more meaningful.

In 1925, a reporter tracked her down to a private hospital in New York. The hospital was run by Dr. Julius Lempert, renowned as a pioneer in otic surgery. Lempert was also known as a financial backer for many Broadway plays, which may be how Suratt met him. She worked with children in his hospital. The reporter found her sitting on a hammock surrounded by children and a prancing monkey. She was quietly telling them stories. Suratt wore a light-pink uniform, as used in England because the color appeared to calm children. She seemed matured, her body a bit fuller. She reluctantly agreed to an interview with the reporter.

"For years I have wanted to do this—to be about children, to take care of them, to study them." She told of helping take care of her younger siblings and that she had looked after children of friends or strangers over the years. "I have the urge to do something that is helpful to someone." Others on the staff said she had an "amazing way with kids." She was first to arrive and the last to leave.

Suratt predicted that she would stay at least through the summer and perhaps return to the stage. She told him she had offers to return to vaudeville, although she called it a "funny and artificial" life. "I was never starstruck. I had a natural stage presence…stayed with it for years…it never penetrated very far into my private life." She was happier now, she told him.

Valeska Suratt never returned to the stage. Instead, she delved deeper into religious studies, often tinged with a bent for mysticism. She studied and wrote essays and tracts about her search. Perhaps appropriately for someone who was often portrayed as a vamp, she studied and wrote about Mary Magdalene. Her focus on Mary Magdalene would lead to her last flash of celebrity and end any chance of a return to entertainment should she indeed wish that life again.

In 1928, she sued some of the most powerful men in Hollywood for plagiarism. Suratt claimed that the script of C.B. DeMille's *King of Kings* was lifted from her screenplay about Mary Magdalene. She sued DeMille, who never deigned to answer the subpoena, and the Motion Picture Producers and Distributors of America. The latter group was headed by a fellow Hoosier, the homely, jug-eared, long-nosed politician Will Hays, who was in effect Hollywood's moral watchdog. The suit was thrown out of the court in 1930, with the judge reportedly saying that Suratt had plagiarized Matthew, Mark, Luke and John. There may have been a small out-of-court settlement just to end the matter. It was said that Suratt was then blacklisted, which seems likely, as DeMille was still angry about the suit twenty years later.

Thus began Suratt's years of obscurity. In 1938, she was living in the house of famed comedienne Fanny Brice, who was portrayed by Barbra Streisand in *Funny Girl*. That same year, the "flaming haired Suratt was an instrument of fate in the life of Mrs. Chanler." Julia Chanler was married to Lewis Stuyvesant Chanler, an Astor descendant who served as lieutenant governor of New York. Suratt and Chanler were working on an unidentified script. Suratt was an influence in Chanler's spiritual quest. She introduced her to Mirza Ahmad Sohrab, who claimed to be a direct descendant of the Prophet Muhammad. Sohrab was a Bahá'í who once served as secretary to 'Abdu'l Bahá, who was considered one of the three central figures in the religion. Sohrab was cowriter of Suratt's Mary Magdalene script.

After that, Suratt's name all but disappears from the newspapers. The only mention of her was of the "Where Are They Now" variety. She was forgotten. She continued her spiritual quests, amassing a large library and writing her essays. She died in poverty in Washington, D.C., four days after her eightieth birthday. She finally returned to Terre Haute to be buried at Highland Lawn Cemetery.

Hautean Hollywood

Hollywood has become so entrenched in the public mind that many do not realize there was a time when movies were made elsewhere.

In February 1913, the *Terre Haute Tribune* announced that "the first moving picture ever written, constructed and posed for in Terre Haute," would soon hit local theaters. It was the brainchild of Robert W. Nicholson, a local film projectionist. Entranced by "moving pictures," Nicholson built his own movie camera, the only one in the city. He decided to try his hand at moviemaking.

He wrote the screenplay for a movie to be called *The Girl in the Tower*. It was a "damsel in distress" melodrama featuring many elements of the cliffhangers that would later become so popular in Hollywood serials. Acting as the film's director, Nicholson began shooting the film in December 1912 with local actors. They shot exteriors at various railroad yards around the city. He rented the Lints & Cornwall artistic studio to film the interiors. The studio on Ohio Street was the only building with a skylight large enough to provide sufficient light for filming.

Nicholson understood early on the Hollywood maxim that you needed a star in your film to be successful. He cast local legend George Mahare in one of the lead roles. Mahare was a farmer turned musician with many talents. He could sing and dance and was adept at mimicry. After performing in local theater productions, where he excelled in comic roles, he turned professional. He spent more than twenty years with touring theater companies and in vaudeville.

The plot of this "railroad play" was a simple one. The villains, for hazy reasons, were intent on sabotaging railroad trains. To carry out their foul deed, they sneakily took over a railroad signal tower. Once inside, they found the only person there was a young female telegraph operator. They were not about to let a mere girl foil their plan. They surprised her and tied her to a chair as they went about their dastardly business. But the girl, played by Katherine Scott, was a plucky lass. She pushed herself across the tower until she reached the telegraph. Then, using her nose, she tapped out an SOS message for help.

Discovering her betrayal of their plot, they grabbed the spunky girl, took her down and tied her to the tracks. Then they "secrete themselves prepared to gloat as their victim is ground to pieces" by an oncoming freight train. But just as the looming hulk of the engine was making for the struggling girl, her heroes rescued her. The villains are then captured and turned over the police. Curses, foiled again. The plot device of a girl tied to the tracks, of course, became a staple in films and cartoons. Interestingly, it is most associated in the minds of many with the Perils of Pauline movies, which were not filmed until the next year. However, being tied to railroad tracks was not among the dangers faced by Pauline.

The film was a success and played at several theaters. Nicholson then took on a project bankrolled by local saloon keeper and theater owner Roy Dycus and his grandly named Dycus Film Company. Dycus put up $600 for a film to be called *The Boy and the Bandit*. This time, the screenplay was written by nineteen-year-old Grover Jones. A miner's son from West Terre Haute, Grover would move to Hollywood and become an Oscar winner and the highest-paid screenwriter in Tinseltown. (For the complete story of Grover Jones, see the author's 2017 book, *Til the Coal Train Hauled It Away*.)

The thin plot involved a bandit and a greedy landlord seeking to take the titular boy's family home. Eventually, the boy captures the bandit and uses $500 reward to save the family homestead. It was filmed in a studio at Third and Ohio and on location at the county fairgrounds (present site of Memorial Stadium) in May 1913. Like many moviemakers, they ran out of money before it was finished. That did not stop them from exhibiting it though. The unfinished film was shown at several theaters in town. Although the Dycus Company announced that further films were forthcoming, there was no further mention of them in the local papers.

Then along came the *The Mysterious Tribune Girl* in 1915. A silhouette of a masked girl appeared on the bottom of the front page of the June 13 edition of the *Terre Haute Tribune*. Readers were informed that the *The Mysterious Tribune Girl* was a five-episode serial that would be shown at the Orpheum Theater in the coming weeks. Not only that, but readers could also win prizes. The paper promised fifty dollars in gold to the "movie fan offering first solution of the mystery" and twenty-five dollars each to the fan who solved the mystery surrounding the girl and for the best suggestion for the storyline of the fifth episode. In essence, it was an early interactive movie experience.

The film was being produced by the Emnkay Studios located in Terre Haute. It offered what were called photo-dramas for advertising purposes. The studio approached chambers of commerce in various cities and offered to film a romantic drama for advertising purposes. The film would highlight various firms and aspects of the city, use local casts and broaden the audience base by filming some scenes in other towns. They already had done productions for Dayton, Ohio, and Memphis.

The first chapter of the serial began with a stylish woman getting off a Big Four train in Terre Haute. A mask covers all of her face except "a pair of lustrous eyes, a row of shining teeth, and a well-rounded chin." She gets in a chauffeur-driven car and is taken to the Deming Hotel. Naturally, word soon spreads of the mystery girl, and the *Tribune* sends its entertainment editor, Mique O'Brien (as himself), to interview her. She does not reveal her identity but tells him that she is in town on an important mission and thus must hide her face.

Later, she has her chauffeur take her shopping in downtown Terre Haute. As she enters Swope & Nehf's jewelry store on Wabash Avenue, a tall, dark man, Duke Dyson, looks on. After he sees her pull a wad of bills out to pay for the jewelry, Dyson confers with the chauffeur. As soon as the girl gets in the car, a hand covers her mouth, while the other grabs the jewelry box. "Head to Indianapolis" is Dyson's command. They speed off.

A *Trib* reporter named Remington just happens to be walking east on Cherry Street when he sees the speeding car with a struggling girl in it go by. His reporter instincts kick in, and he flags down a motorcycle cop appropriately named Speed Hough. After informing the police station to send out a bulletin, Speed tells the reporter to hop on the back, and the intrepid pair roar off in pursuit.

The chase speeds along Wabash Avenue. With the car sputtering in front of Highland Lawn Cemetery, Dyson tosses the jewelry box away and jumps out of the car, leaving the fainting girl and chauffeur behind to face the police.

While Speed takes off after Dyson, the reporter goes to the aid of the girl, only to come face to face with a .45 revolver pulled by Demon, the chauffer. The policeman catches up with Dyson atop a railroad trestle. After a struggle, Dyson tosses Hough off the trestle. Luckily, the policeman is able grab hold of a rail and is dangling there. When Remington goes to aid the struggling Speed, Dyson runs back to the car, and they head east to Brazil.

On the alert for the fleeing car, a Brazil cop stops the car and pulls out Dyson. Just as Remington and Speed arrive, they hear the girl say, "Release him; I refuse to prosecute. He is my ---." She gets in the car with Dyson, and they head back to Terre Haute, leaving a stunned pair of rescuers behind.

The second chapter features the *Tribune*. Surprised by the girl's refusal to prosecute, the reporter still knows that he has a good story. He rushes back to the *Tribune* office to write up the tale and put it out on the newswire. The audience then gets a glimpse of how newspapers were made, following the process through typesetting and printing. The result is the headline "Auto Bandit May Go Free—Mysterious Tribune Girl Refuses to Press Charges." The scene dissolves to a lonely newsboy named Tommy Williams. Tommy is family's main provider, as his dad is a feckless drunk who doesn't support the family. He is in tears because he hasn't sold any papers. Then a big car pulls up. A kindly masked lady buys all his papers and offers to take him home.

The third chapter is one long plucking of the heart strings. In the car, Tommy tells the girl his sad story. He is helping to support his hardworking mother, who struggles to keep food on the table for Tommy and his many siblings. To make things worse, his baby brother is seriously ill. Even when he has money from selling papers, his dad sometimes takes it from him and heads to the saloon. As they near his humble home, they see Tommy's father stumbling home drunk. Spying Tommy, Mr. Williams tries to pull him from the car. Tommy runs into the house to proudly show the family the money he has made. Just then, his dad rushes in, and steals the money. Mr. Williams heads out to spend the money at a local saloon.

Wonder of wonders, the reporter Remington just happens to be walking along the street and forces the wayward father to return home. As they reach the house, a kindly local doctor emerges from the house. "Your child is dead," he tells Williams.

Several weeks later, Tommy is seen hunting for rabbits at Highland Lawn when he spots a jewelry box hidden in the grass. Realizing that it is expensive and he could sell it to help his family, he heads back to town. Out of nowhere, Duke Dyson appears and grabs the box. Again, Remington and Speed are in the right place at the right time. They see Dyson hop a freight train headed for Clinton. While Remington jumps on an interurban car going to Clinton, Speed returns to the police station to warn the Clinton cops to be on the lookout for Dyson. Hearing the news, the mystery girl says that she won't protect Dyson this time. In her hotel room, she takes off her mask and slumps onto the bed. Her "tear-stained cheeks" and "quivering lips indicated the sorrow Dyson's latest escapade had brought her."

The fourth chapter opens with rather surreal scenes. As Dyson is dodging the Clinton police among boxcars, he sees a figure that may or not be Charlie Chaplin. "Charlie" is eating a bean sandwich and picking his teeth with a railroad spike. Then Dyson sees Remington approaching and draws a gun. As he is aiming at the reporter, his mind is flooded with visions of his old home, saintly mother and jail cells. Remington knocks the gun away and takes him back to Terre Haute. Once again, the mystery girl appears and begs police not to jail him. This time, her pleas do no good. They thrust Dyson into a cell.

The fifth chapter was written by the winner of the contest to choose the final episode. A letter lands on Remington's desk at the *Trib*. "Am called to mother at my country home. You must visit me and I will tell all. Can offer Mr. Williams a job—Miss Tribune." Remington persuades Williams to make a trip to the farm. Mystery Girl takes Remington to a secluded spot on the farm and tells him her story. She is a well-known movie actress who returned home when her mother told her that her brother, Duke Dyson, had left the farm and led a dissolute life. She donned the masked to prevent the public and Dyson from knowing her identity. A lovestruck Remington returns to Terre Haute and succeeds in having the charges against Dyson dismissed. Seeing the error of his ways, Dyson returns to the farm with Remington. They all lived happily ever after.

With that, moviemaking in Terre Haute faded to black.

We'll Make You a Star, Kid

A columnist in the *Van Nuys Reporter* of December 20, 1934, breathlessly announced that the Van Nuys City Hall had received a visit from a young Paramount movie star named Billy Lee. Four-year-old Billy, described as "a handsome little chap…with an irresistible smile" and an amazing conversationalist, was there with his family to visit an old friend from his hometown, West Terre Haute, Indiana.

In 1930, the Schlensker family lived just off National Avenue in West Terre Haute. The father, Pete, was a sometime farmer and miner (and ten-year minor-league baseball player), while mom Stella looked after the children, three sons and a daughter. By 1934, the family (at least mom, dad and the two youngest boys) were living on Klump Avenue in Van Nuys. All in all, it was a world away from West Terre Haute. Why they left is uncertain, but one can surmise that they were part of that stream who thought the answer to surviving the Depression was out west. As the mines played out and West Terre Haute's decline was hastened by the Depression, many of its citizens left the area. (West Terre Haute lost approximately one-fourth of its population between 1928 and 1940.) The Shlenskers joined the exodus (oldest children Charles and Lucille remained behind) in 1933.

There is no evidence that the family was previously involved in the entertainment business (in his obituary, it was said that Pete claimed to have taught Billy to dance). They were a simple farm family from Indiana. It is known that Billy showed talent, appearing in church productions as a toddler. His first real stage performance took place in Terre Haute in 1932.

Not yet four years old, he took the stage in the Tribune-Star Christmas Frolic in 1932. Singing and dancing in front of a miniature stage set built by his father, he did a minstrel-esque routine in blackface, singing "Old Black Joe." He was a hit. In true Hollywood myth fashion, it is said that a talent scout for Paramount saw or heard of his dazzling debut and offered him a contract.

Flash-forward to Hollywood. Pete and Stella enrolled young Billy in a private school in Los Angeles. There, teacher Ethel Meglin quickly recognized Billy's talents and enthusiasm and trained him in singing and dancing. With her help and with his father acting as his agent, Billy, now known professionally as Billy Lee, was signed to a contract by Paramount Studios. Over the next decade, he was to appear in more than forty movies, ranging from westerns with Randolph Scott, Gene Autry and Roy Rogers to musicals (Billy was an accomplished drummer). In one musical, *Reg'lar Fellers*, Billy appears with Carl Switzer, who had played Alfalfa in the Our Gang comedies and, coincidently, was born just across the state line from West Terre Haute in the West Union/Marshall area. Billy was recognized as a genuinely talented performer.

Adorable Billy Lee made his last movie in 1943. Like many child stars, the ebbing of his youth also saw the waning of his career. By age fourteen, his movie career was over. Billy and the family returned to West Terre Haute, living on North Sixth Street. Always precocious for his age, Billy tried to marry at age sixteen. In the spring of 1946, he applied for a license to marry a Garfield High School graduate named Peggy Frew, eighteen. The license was denied by a Vigo County Circuit Court judge because of his age. Only later that year were the couple allowed to marry. Then, the same judge who had earlier denied the license because he thought it only "puppy love" was convinced that "they were that way about each other" and issued the license after both parents gave their consent. However, by that time Billy and Margaret had crossed the county line and were married in Brazil, Indiana, in February. He listed his job as truck driver.

At the time of the marriage, Billy (who had been attending Concannon High School and working at Stran Steel) told a reporter that he still had a few months to go on his contract and hoped that Hollywood would welcome his talents again. Hollywood did not call.

The couple moved in 1947 to Muncie, Indiana, where Billy found a job at the Kiser Plating and Jewelry Company. Billy enlisted in the army in October 1947. Evidently, their "puppy love" did not survive the moves, as the couple divorced in 1948. Margaret would remarry a man from Muncie in 1949.

Billy was discharged in February 1950 but reenlisted in 1951 and served in the Korean War. The Internet Movie Database (IMDb) credits Billy with appearing in two 1952 movies, one with Charlie Chaplin and the other starring Elizabeth Taylor. In both, his role was listed as only "little boy." However, as Billy was a twenty-two-year-old soldier in Korea, it is likely the database confused him with another child actor named Billy Lee Aimone.

Following his discharge in 1953, Billy settled in California. He may have played several bit parts in some television anthology series in 1954, but the evidence for that is scant. He held different jobs until his death in 1989. Friends and neighbors said that he never mentioned his earlier movie career and was just a "reg'ler feller."

No matter his end, Billy left behind his movie appearances as a legacy. Several, like *Wagons West* and *Biscuit Eater*, are available on DVD. Young, charming, four-year-old Billy Lee still lives on celluloid, now digitized for the ages.

Awful Crimes

A Lynching on the Wabash

Ida Finkelstein was a young teacher. At this time in American history, the role of women as teachers of the young was well established. Such young women were underpaid but dedicated and admired for what they did. She taught at the Elm Grove School in northeastern Terre Haute. Originally from Lafayette, she had taken the teachers course at Indiana State Normal. Slender, longhaired and only twenty, Ida boarded with a local family. She made forty-five dollars per month during the school year, sending all but five dollars per month to Chicago to help her mother and sisters.

February 25, 1901, was an ordinary Monday for Ida. The first part of the school day was spent getting her students to focus on their work again after the weekend break. She then settled in to teach. After the children had gone home, she stayed behind to tidy up the school. Her workday ended around 4:00 p.m., and she set off for home. She always rode the interurban to and from school. The track was about a mile from the school through a wooded area.

Earlier in the day, a man had gone to a doctor's office to get medicine for his child. The doctor thought that the man was acting strangely, as if he was "on the verge of mania of some kind." At 2:30 p.m., the man put on his hunting jacket and boarded the interurban, exiting at the Fruitridge Avenue stop near the Hulman farm. He pulled his hunting coat close around him and headed into the woods.

Around 5:30 p.m., Ida was found crawling to a nearby house. She was bloodied. Dr. Weinstein was called and rushed to the scene. She was taken to Union Hospital, where she soon died. Before her death, she was conscious long enough to describe her attacker as a tall, light-skinned black man wearing a hunting coat.

By the next morning, Terre Haute police were frantically searching for the killer. Any attack on a young woman was cause for alarm, but an assault on a young white woman by a black man was a decided affront in the minds of many. The ugly, fraught racial divide in America made it so. Black men across the city were questioned. Every man of color encountered was looked at with suspicion. Finally, a local "colored man" told police that he knew who the killer was. Deputies went to a local car works and arrested George Ward, a forty-year-old laborer. Ward protested his innocence but was visibly shaken. He was taken to the county jail, hard by the Wabash River.

Even as the police and sheriff were questioning him, word of Ward's arrest was sweeping the streets like wildfire: a "nigger" had raped and killed that poor teacher. There was no evidence indicating that Ida had been sexually assaulted. On street corners and alleys, groups of men gathered. Something should be done, they fumed.

Meanwhile, at the jail, Ward soon confessed to the crime. He had come across Ida at about 5:30 p.m. He was walking behind her. Sensing him, he said, the fearful young teacher turned and called out, "Don't walk behind me. If you are going my way, walk in front of me." Ward said that he was doing as she asked, but as he came abreast with her, Finkelstein called him a "dirty nigger" and slapped him on the face. She began to run away. Enraged, Ward raised his double-barreled shotgun and shot her in the back of the head. She crumpled facedown on the ground. He walked to her trembling body and, pulling out his hunting knife, raised her head and cut her throat. His knife blade broke off in her neck.

The idle men and fevered talk on the streets of Terre Haute soon turned into a mob with vengeance on its collective mind. Shortly after noon, a few members of the mob forced their way into the jail. They were repelled, but it was now certain that reinforcements were needed. All deputies and volunteers were called in to help with a possible siege of the jail. Sheriff Fasig contacted Indiana governor Winfield Durbin. The governor agreed that the situation was perilous and ordered elements of the Indiana National Guard to proceed to Terre Haute.

Ward was taken to a cell as plans were made to transfer him to Indianapolis for his own safety. It was too late. As Ward sat in his cell smoking his corncob pipe, he could hear the howling mob. People assembled from all over the county and surrounded the jail. The crowd, in possession now of a heavy timber post, surged forward. The two ostensible leaders were strangers on crutches. The doors were battered open. A vanguard of angry men spewed into the jail and headed for the cells.

They found the terrified Ward hiding in a bathtub, a hammock drawn over him offering feeble protection. Angry arms reached for him, pulling him out of the hiding place. One of the leaders shouted, "Hurry up; your time is short, and you had better pray for your soul." As they pulled him out of the cell, Ward tried banging his head on the wall in a vain attempt to commit suicide before the crowd could do its worst to him.

As he was pushed into the jail office, Ward could see a rabid crowd of men and boys. Some of them held hammers. A local blacksmith stepped forward, his fearsome hammer in hand, and struck Ward's head as he would when shaping a piece of iron. The blow likely killed Ward instantly (he was also knifed in the face), but his death was not enough punishment for the crowd. They wanted more in retribution from Ward for his sins.

Two rope halters were obtained from Chisler's stable (the men who took them generously told Chisler that they would be returned to him later). Ward was taken to the Wabash River drawbridge. A piece of chain was pulled from the bridge. The chain and ropes were fashioned into a gallows and noose. Ward's dead body was hung from the bridge. A crowd estimated at more than two thousand people (including prominent citizens and, later, schoolgirls) watched Ward dangle in the winds above the Wabash. At times, his scarred face looked toward West Terre Haute.

Still, it was not enough. A few hardy souls pulled Ward down from the bridge. Fuel was obtained. A funeral pyre was made along the riverbank. People surged forward to watch his body burn down to its essence. Eventually, those sated by the savage end of George Ward, satisfied that elemental justice had been done, drifted back to their homes.

A few diehards remained behind, scurrying for mementos. One enterprising man was selling Ward's skeletal toes for a dollar apiece. A twelve-year-old boy proudly showed off his treasure: a shred of Ward's clothing, a charred bone and a piece of the hangmen's rope.

The looters who scavenged what little remained of George Ward had barely made off with their ghoulish souvenirs before word of the lynching spread. Thanks to the telegraph and phone, news of the "event" appeared in newspapers across the country. Even the *New York Times* reported the actions of a mob in Terre Haute. Rumor and hearsay were swift currents flooding the streets and dirt roads of Vigo County.

Opposite, top: The body of George Ward hangs from the Wabash River Bridge. *Vigo County Historical Society*.

Opposite, bottom: *Vigo County Historical Society*.

Above: Lynching was not enough vengeance for the crowd. Ward's body was consigned to a funeral pyre. *Vigo County Historical Society*.

But who was this George Ward, who went from being just another ignored black man to a figure of infamy? There is very little to go on. It was said he was born in Kentucky. Estimates of his age ranged from twenty-seven to forty. He could have been the George Ward who was born in Kentucky, but one report said that he confided in a jailer that his name was really Robinson. It was said that Ward had spent time in an insane asylum or perhaps was responsible for the earlier murder of a white man found in a Terre Haute alley.

At some point, he or his family moved to Circleville, Ohio. His Sunday school teacher there recalled that he was a good boy, and she was shocked at what he had become. He came to Terre Haute around 1896. He was once a servant for the Erlich family in Seelyville. He was fired when he was found lurking under the bed of one of their young daughters. He claimed, oddly, that he was under the bed because he was looking for a drink of water.

It was likely around this time that he met Ruth Roberts. Ruth was from the free black settlement in Lost Creek Township. Ruth had married George in 1897 or 1898. (She may have been the sweetheart whom others later noted George had been abusive to after church services.) At the time of the lynching, the couple had a three-year-old son and an infant daughter. The 1900 city directory listed them as living at 1610 Spruce Street and George as a laborer at the railroad car works in Terre Haute.

George had never had any serious trouble with the police, only a minor larceny charge. Some said that he was a petty thief. A storekeeper where Ward traded said they kept an eye on him when he was in the store and always made him pay cash for purchases. Coworkers at the car shop viewed him as good-natured, but things were wont to disappear when he was around. They also noted he was "a fool for women" and was always talking about them. Ruth reported that he seemed quite normal the night after the murder. He ate a hearty supper and went to bed. It was not until the next day that she heard of the arrest. She avowed that he had never been in an insane asylum.

The lynching occupied the news for weeks afterward. One newspaper reported that Ruth Ward was going to auction off her husband's hunting coat and shotgun. Another noted that some of the items would be displayed at a local store. These reports were later denied, but others sought to profit from the tragedy. James Huffman, a railroad conductor and a spectator at the lynching, proudly showed a piece of the rope as proof he was there.

Outrage against Ward mingled with sympathy for Ida Finkelstein and her family. Ida's mother, prostrate with grief, had taken refuge with her brother,

Meyer Levin. It was noted that Ida's death left the family destitute. Benefits for the family were held in Lafayette and Terre Haute. Citizens contributed to the fund. Within weeks, more than $500 was raised for the family. One man offered that if every one of the two to three thousand people who reportedly witnessed the lynching contributed a dollar, the family would be well cared for. Also destitute, according to Ruth's father, were Ward's widow and children. No benefits were staged for them.

The tragedy continued to reverberate. George Wood, a man who had witnessed the lynching, reportedly went insane from the vicious spectacle. Crazed, he turned himself in to the Vigo County Jail. Wardens there soon transferred him to an asylum. African Americans feared that even more white retribution for Ward's crime would follow. It was noted that many were quietly leaving Terre Haute for Brazil, Indiana, or other safer havens. Whites also feared more trouble when word spread that Ward's brother had arrived in Terre Haute on his own personal search for revenge.

One of the more absurd aspects of the lynching was the official dithering over what, if anything, remained of George Ward's body. Vigo County coroner James Willis announced that he could not as yet determine the location of Ward's death. Was it Harrison Township, where Terre Haute was located, or Sugar Creek Township, containing West Terre Haute? The decision was an important one, it seemed, because where he died would determine which township would be charged with burial costs. As there was said to be almost nothing of Ward's body that had not been burned or looted, it seems a moot point. What may have happened was that the slim remains were buried in Terre Haute's potters' field or, irony of ironies, burned in the city crematorium located along the river, just yards from where the lynching took place.

And what of justice for Ward's lynching? It was announced that a grand jury would convene on March 11 to look into the case and "undertake to learn the names of the lynchers." There was hope that the ringleaders would be identified and punished. After meeting, the jurors returned no indictments. Some were disgusted that the crime would go "unsolved," but others were glad to have the ordeal at some sort of official end. Still others thought that the fix was in—it was said that two men who were added late to the grand jury had already made public statements supporting the lynching.

Of course, reaction to the lynching was headline news. Editorials and newspaper stories from around Indiana and the nation condemned the savagery of lynching. There were calls to strengthen Indian's anti-lynching law. An editorial in the *Indianapolis Sun* posited that one of the reasons the lynching occurred was that the people of Vigo County had so little faith in the county's leaders or justice system.

The opinions of local leaders were eagerly sought by the newspapers. Most actively condemned the lynching as inhuman and a blight on the city. But as the *Terre Haute Gazette* noted, a lot of "ifs" and "buts" were used. It was almost if they were saying it was all Ward's fault.

But those who thought that justice had been done were plentiful and vocal. One E.W. Leeds noted, "When sure of his man Judge Lynch is a wise and just judge." A former city councilman named Hebb was of the opinion that "the mob did right. The only mistake was killing the wretch before they burned him." There were many who shared that opinion. Among them, curiously, was Reverend A.M. Taylor of the AME church in Rockville, Indiana, who believed that "hell-deserving wretches" like Ward deserved their fate.

Much ink was spread over the Ward lynching, but one such statement that catches the eye was printed the night of the lynching. The *Terre Haute Gazette* opined that "Terre Haute is the chief victim of the murder of the Negro murderer Ward."

That's right, *Terre Haute* was the victim—not Ida Finkelstein and not George Ward.

FLAT IRON MURDERS

There was something not quite right about Vernie Alfonso Lewis—at least, that's what some thought. Maybe it was his eyes, some said. Something about those eyes. Maybe it was the way he acted, sort of goofy or slow. But there was something. Anyway, he was known as that "little, deformed, abnormal looking fellow."

Vernie was born in 1880 in Needmore, Indiana, just south of Clinton, to Franklin and Elizabeth Hull Lewis. He was not that good in school. He left after the third grade and went to work in the coal mines, including some in Sugar Creek. His father died when Vernie was only thirteen years old.

Life was a struggle for Vernie. He shuttled between jobs as a miner or laborer, lived sometimes in Needmore and at other times in West Terre Haute or Terre Haute. He married seventeen-year-old Ida Shepherd in 1902. They had a son named Vernie. Preferring the company of another man, Ida divorced him in 1905, taking their son with her. A year later, he remarried, this time to Frances Chunn. Things did not go well for the couple.

Like Ida, Frances found Vernie hard to deal with and left him for another man. By 1915, Vernie Lewis was living in Terre Haute with his mother.

Lizzie Blacketer lived in a shotgun house on North Seventeenth Street in Terre Haute, just south of Lost Creek. The Murray and Balding families lived north of her. As usual, Lizzie woke early on Monday, March 15, 1915. The papers carried news of the war raging in Europe. As she went outside her modest home, she was a bit surprised how quiet the Balding home was. Usually there was a whirlwind of activity there as the children got ready for school or play. Not wishing to pry but worried that something was wrong, Lizzie went reluctantly to the silent house. Stepping on the porch, she saw eight-year-old Merion Celeste Balding on the front room floor. She lay in a pillow of her own blood.

By now, Lizzie was frantic. She ran next door to tell her friend Mamie Murray about what she saw. They rushed to a neighbor, who called the Terre Haute police. Officer Smith hurried to the house on his bicycle. When Smith arrived, he stepped into a horrific scene. The policeman had seen some bad things in his time, but this was just about the worst.

He was greeted by the sight of the dead young girl. Near her was the body of her brother Clifford. Smith could see into the bedroom of the shotgun house. There were more bodies. There in the bed was the mother, Mary Balding; her baby, Walter, was in her arms. Beside her was three-year-old Irene. Sprawled across their feet was another son, Thomas, who was dead. Smith rang for an ambulance and detectives. Looking around, he saw two flat irons covered in blood.

The ambulance attendants found that Mary Balding, Clifford, Irene and Walter were still alive. Mary and Walter subsequently died at St. Anthony Hospital.

Frank Fedderson was a well-known and accomplished detective. He and his colleagues did what all police should do. They began interviewing the neighbors. They learned that husband and father William Balding worked as a lineman for Bell Telephone. He had been in Centralia, Illinois, for nearly a month but was expected home soon. As usual, they asked if there had been any problems between the Baldings and others. Did they have any reason to believe that the Baldings had enemies who might wish to harm them?

The neighbors immediately cast suspicion on two men: Ira Tobey and Garley Stevens. They were well-known troublemakers and rowdies who often roamed drunkenly through the neighborhood. Tobey was immediately arrested. Stevens could not be found. When they heard he might be in Whitcomb Heights, the police headed across the Wabash to find him. They were told he was not there but was expected back; they left a message that they were looking for him. The next day, Stevens dutifully called the police and was told to come to the jail. When he arrived, the detectives discovered he had a series of fresh cuts on his hand. The police were hopeful that they had their murderers.

That same day, the name of Vernie Lewis, who was known to visit the Baldings, came out. Vernie, they learned, was Lizzie Blacketer's son. They returned to North Seventeenth Street to interview Lizzie. She told them that Vernie had gone to bed with the rest of the family around 7:00 p.m. As far as she knew, he had not left the house. They tracked Vernie to the Cloelle mine near West Terre Haute. He claimed that his mother was telling them the truth. He had gone to bed early and slept all night. The detectives continued to investigate the crime. By Friday, they concurred that Tobey and Steven's alibis were genuine.

Police carried on. Later Friday, they were told by someone that two men who lived a few blocks away might have important information for them. First thing Saturday morning, Fedderson interviewed George Wheatstein and James Unsel, who told him that contrary to what Vernie Lewis had said, he had been in their homes after 7:00 p.m. Unsel noted that Vernie—who was normally a happy, cheerful person—was acting very strangely. He left Unsel's house about 10:00 p.m. It cast doubt on Vernie's testimony and immediately made him the prime suspect for the atrocities.

That morning, the detectives returned to the mine. They asked the mine boss to get Vernie for them under some pretext that would not alarm him. The boss said that would be no problem, as he had already "jacked up" Vernie because he had been acting very oddly and shirking work. The boss descended into the mine, returning to the surface about fifteen minutes later with Vernie in tow.

They arrested Vernie. He said he stuck by his alibi but would be glad to go to the jail and tell them everything he knew about the case. The suspect and the detectives exchanged uncomfortable small talk on the long drive to the Terre Haute jail.

Vernie continued to proclaim his innocence throughout the morning. He finally did admit that he had left his house without his mother knowing and had visited Wheatstein and Unsel. Returning Vernie to his cell, Fedderson and his colleague drove up to the Blacketer home. They found blood on the side door of the house. They searched the home and found Vernie's pants and suspenders. They too were bloodstained.

On Sunday, Fedderson again interviewed Vernie. Once more, Vernie swore that he was not guilty. Fedderson was frustrated but had an idea. On Monday, he had Vernie moved to a cell in the jail's hospital ward. Fedderson had himself locked alone in the cell with Vernie, telling the jailer not to let anyone else near them. He found Vernie sobbing uncontrollably on the bed. Fedderson spoke with him softly but persistently, quietly hammering questions at him about the crime, not allowing Vernie time to himself.

Around 1:30 p.m., Vernie just hung his head, saying nothing for minutes. Then he looked up and began crying again. Finally, without looking at the detective, Vernie said, "Oh god, it was awful. It was awful." Fedderson tried to calm the prisoner and asked him to make his confession. Vernie looked up, his face ashen and pallid, but said nothing.

Fedderson leaned back and asked Vernie to imagine it was his family, his wife and children, who had been brutally slain while he was out of town. How would he feel? Vernie sobbed and cried out, "Oh, don't say anymore. My God don't let the mob get to me, for I know they will if they find it out. They will tear me to pieces and, oh, I don't want to go to the electric chair, but I can't help it now." And then he cried out his "motive" for the bloodshed. "I could not bear to see them move away from the neighborhood. It preyed on my mind as long as I could stand for it to."

Again, Fedderson asked him to make a formal confession. Vernie said he would, but only if the police got him out of Terre Haute so he would not be lynched. Fedderson promised he would tell only his partner and the prosecutor and would immediately get Vernie away from town if he confessed. He then launched into his story.

After visiting Wheatstein and Unsel, he returned to North Seventeenth at about 9:30 p.m. or so. Going to the Baldings's, he pushed aside a piece of carpeting covering a broken window. He picked up two flat irons from the kitchen and went to the bedroom. Mary Balding was still awake, but before she could speak, he began battering her with blows. How many, he could not remember. He then struck Thomas and Irene. Moving to the front room, Clifford spoke to him, but Vernie could not recall what he said. He then struck Clifford and Celeste.

He then returned to the kitchen to wash his hands, climbed back out the window to his own home and snuck into his bed. It was over. Fedderson then left to arrange the transfer.

Fedderson knew that Vernie's concerns for his safety were real. They both remembered the story of George Ward being taken from the jail by a mob and hanged from the Wabash River Bridge. After telling his partner,

Armstrong, the two went to Deputy Sheriff Katzenbach, who gave them a car to transport Vernie to Indianapolis for his protection.

The detectives took off along US 40 to drive to Indianapolis, with Vernie cowering in the back. They constantly looked over their shoulders to see if they were being tailed. Just as they passed Greencastle, a tire blew out. It took more than an hour to fix the puncture, an hour that seemed endless as they scanned the road for signs of a lynching party. But they made it, depositing Vernie in jail and returning to Terre Haute without incident.

Vernie gave out further information. He loved Mary Balding. In his fevered mind, she loved him too. He was "insanely jealous" of her. He wanted her all to himself. His love for her was driving him mad. He also told that he had been struck in the head in a mine accident. Since then, he said, thoughts of murder had preyed on his mind. That is why an innocent family was brutally bludgeoned by a pathetic, delusional man.

As Vernie confessed, there was no jury trial. The courts had psychiatrists interview him to determine he if he was insane. There were mixed reports. Eventually, Vernie Lewis accepted a verdict of first-degree murder and was sentenced to life in prison on September 17, 1915.

The next day, he was taken to the state penitentiary in Michigan City. His mother accompanied him on his trip to prison. His admission record showed he was thirty-five years old, of medium stature and in fair health. His mental condition was described as feeble-minded, and he was considered a sexual pervert. It noted he was a Methodist and had left home at age sixteen. His only previous arrest had been in Clinton on a charge of intoxication. Vernie began his life sentence.

After serving twenty-five years, he applied for parole, but it was denied. From 1943 to 1945, he was admitted at least ten times to Robert Long Hospital in Indianapolis to be treated for various illnesses. In 1945, he was given parole by the governor, with the stipulation that he must live in Missouri. Missouri was likely chosen because his brother lived in Poplar Bluff, and Vernie was paroled in his care. Vernie Lewis died in 1961. He lived forty-six years longer than his four innocent victims. And what of those bereaved left behind after the murder? Father and husband William Balding eventually remarried twice. He died in 1967. Clifford died in the same year as his mother's killer. Irene died in 1973, leaving behind a loving family.

DEATH CRY OF THE GYPSY

On May 1, 1914, about thirty gypsies (Romani is the more proper term) moving north from their winter quarters in Kentucky set up camp in West Terre Haute. They set about fortune telling, horse trading and trying to sell handmade goods to the locals. The intrepid visited the camp, and the gawkers walked or drove by to catch a glimpse. Shopkeepers maintained a balance between hoping for sales and keeping eagle-eyed surveillance as the gypsies entered their stores.

All in all, it seemed like any other visit by the gypsies. West Terre Haute warily accepted their presence. But Sunday evidently became a bacchanal day at the camp. Over the course of the day and night, eight kegs of beer and other drink were consumed among the thirty. Neighbors reported that the "camp was a scene of brawling and hilarity." Eventually, most, sated with drink, took to their beds. But in the early hours of Monday, one imposing figure still stalked about the camp.

Demetro John (later research noted that his name was more properly Tsina) was a large man with a commanding presence. Born in Brazil, South America, he was a fifty-five-year-old who listed his profession as coppersmith and was considered a leader of the band. Whether John stayed awake drinking while others slept or awoke at some point to return to the bottle is unknown. But by 5:30 a.m., he was likely dwelling on a history of family troubles (he believed his wife, Socca, had been unfaithful) and feeling resentment toward his "in-laws." Around 6:00 a.m., an old woman named Katarina, one of the first up that morning, heard gunshots. Panic spread through the camp as it was learned that John had first bludgeoned and then shot Socca. He then shot her father, Bob Riska, and son-in-law, Joe Riska.

Terrified members ran to a nearby saloon or perhaps a farmhouse (or both) to report the crime. Police from West Terre Haute and Terre Haute responded. Terrified Roma told them to be careful, as Demetro John was still stalking around the camp, still had his gun (a 16 gauge Remington rifle) and promised death to anyone who came near. Cautiously, they maneuvered around. They saw him sitting in front of his tent, gun in hand, thinking of what he had done. Instead of resisting, Old John calmly handed his gun over and meekly surrendered. Police found Socca and Bob already dead and Joe Riska, wearing only half his face, clinging to life by a wisp. They took John to jail in Terre Haute. The next day, Joe died. The "Death Cry of the Gypsy" echoed across Paris Avenue that day and the next in Terre Haute.

After John was taken to jail, the Romani "tribe" gathered to arrange the burial of their dead. The bodies were taken to Hickman's funeral home in Terre Haute. Soon, a man named Steve Miller was summoned from Peoria, Illinois. Terre Haute newspapers conjectured that he was an adopted member of the tribe and related that he "claimed" to be a Freemason in the Chicago lodge and a member of the Odd Fellows in Peoria. Evidently, he acted as a liaison between the Romani and authorities whenever he was needed. The tribe had moved to east of Terre Haute to remove themselves from the death scene.

Miller and tribe members set out to make arrangements for burial. Hickman gladly offered his most expensive casket, and it was eagerly purchased. Soon, the more upscale stores in Terre Haute were visited by the spectacle of exotically attired gypsies shopping for the finest goods available to clothe their dead. Socca, John's murdered wife, was placed in an expensive "silk dress of brilliant colors and oriental design." On her head was wrapped a red silk scarf, her feet covered by red silk hose and leather slippers. Her father, Bob, was clothed in a dark suit and felt hat. Joe was in a light suit, costly Panama hat and tan shoes. Both men were clad in silk underwear. Pipes and tobacco were placed in the coffins. The bodies were covered with white silk sheets. An aged woman broke down, wailing, murmuring John's name while mimicking the signs of a hanging.

On May 16, 1914, the bodies were moved to Highland Lawn Cemetery. At the burial site, "strange balls of incense" were placed around the graves. The caskets were lowered through haloes of smoke, accompanied by the wailings of women and beatings of breasts. When the graves were covered, wine bottles were broken and their contents poured in shapes of a cross on the graves.

In the meantime, John was arraigned in city court on May 8. Despite pleading not guilty, he was charged with murder four days later, with the trial scheduled for September. It was just the start of a two-year process.

After two continuances, it was thought the trial would finally take place in September 1915. Members of the tribe gathered for the event, some staying in a boardinghouse in Terre Haute. The night before the trial, a "babblement" at the boardinghouse led to calls for the police. A row had started in one of the rooms when a supporter of John's trumpeted that he was paying $300 to get him out of jail. Terre Haute police had to push through a curious crowd of Hauteans to enter the house. There they found an uproarious scene of Romani arguing and feuding. Police had to draw their guns in the melee. Finally, they took seven men through the crowd into a waiting paddy wagon and on to jail. After practically the entire station finally calmed the ongoing storm, all but one of the men were released.

The next day at the trial, the Romani were searched before being allowed entry into the courtroom. John sat in a chair surrounded by his son and three deputies. After much legal maneuvering, the case was postponed yet again. "Little" Dick Wereneke, the prosecutor, argued against it, citing costs of once again bringing back witnesses to testify.

The trial was then moved to Rockville, Indiana, in a change of venue requested by the defense. Again, the prosecution had opposed the move, as it would cause difficulty and cost the taxpayers more than $600. In January 1915, the court met in Rockville. The Demetro John who appeared in court was a much reduced man. He had lost sixty pounds, and prison pallor washed his face. Jail had been a psychic and physical assault on a man previously unbound by walls or borders. He was weak. Jailers reported that he had collapsed when being moved from jail to courthouse. They said John "worries about his problems and seldom eats." He claimed his confinement was costly in another way. He entered jail in 1914 with $5,000 in his possession. Now he was broke. The costs of his defense and supporting family had emptied his pockets.

Once again, the trial was postponed. The denouement finally came in April 1916. In a sort of plea bargain, two of the murder charges were dropped and John agreed to plead guilty to the second-degree murder of his wife. On April 20, he was taken to the Indiana State Prison in Michigan City.

At the prison, records noted that John was convicted of second-degree murder and given a life term. He was fifty-eight years old and had been born to G. and Stalca John. He was illiterate, and his mental condition was listed as insane. He was Roman Catholic, and his profession was listed as coppersmith. A brother named Steven, of South Carolina, was listed as next of kin. His wife and other victims lay in a Terre Haute cemetery far from the lands of their births. It has long been noted in Terre Haute that Romani make almost annual pilgrimages to visit the graves.

Prison is hard for anyone, but to a gypsy used to wandering ways, it must have been a brutal life. Fortunately for Demetro John, it was not to last forever. Within eighteen months, and against the wishes of his own board of pardons, Governor Goodrich pardoned him, which has caused many to suspect bribery may have been involved. The parole stated that John had no previous criminal record, was in poor health, bordering on insanity and suffering from locomotor attaxia, which prevented him from walking. He was to be taken back to Brazil by his son to die.

Demetro John was sent abroad "to the *thema*—unspecified foreign land," and there in some unknown place he died.

In Times of War

"One of Those Uncommon Geniuses"

When it was built, it was named Fort Harrison. Later, it was called the Fort of Two Presidents. But the reason it was built was a man named Tecumseh and his quest to save his people.

For Tecumseh it was the same disheartening story for Native Americans. It had been happening to the East and South for nearly two centuries, and then it inexorably moved to the Indiana Territory. The pattern remained the same. First the newcomers came looking for the bounty of the land (furs, gold, timber), then they cast covetous eyes on the land itself. It was preordained that struggles would follow.

The Indiana Territory became one of the most highly charged battlegrounds in those ongoing struggles during the early nineteenth century. The primary antagonists in this drama were Shawnee leader Tecumseh and William Henry Harrison.

Harrison was the scion of an aristocratic Virginia family; his father was a signer of the Declaration of Independence. He was appointed governor of the Indiana Territory in 1801. The ambitious Harrison wanted to be the governor of a state, not just of a mainly unsettled territory. He immediately set out to "negotiate" land cession treaties with Native American groups to open more of Indiana for white settlement. He used whatever methods he needed, including threats and bribery, to get Native Americans to put their signature or "X" on the pieces of paper giving away their lands. At the 1809 Fort Wayne Treaty, it was said that 241 casks of whiskey lubricated the negotiations.

Tecumseh was a Shawnee born in the Ohio Territory in 1768. He and his brother Tenskwatawa (the Prophet) were to become among the most important Native American leaders in history. Both sought to protect tribes from the white onslaught, but in two different ways. The Prophet declared himself the conduit between them and the spirit worlds. He proclaimed himself a seer and a man given visions by the spirits. He preached a nativist message, saying that only by abandoning the white man's ways and returning to their old ways could Native Americans resist the incursions of whites.

Tecumseh was a "global thinker" who knew that the only hope of Native American survival was to give up their fractious ways of the past and join a strong confederation of tribes. He traveled thousands of miles and worked tirelessly to convince native nations across the East and South to join a confederation. Tecumseh is one of the least appreciated Americans in history. Were he white, he would rank with Jefferson, Washington or any other founder.

Even his adversary, William Henry Harrison, admired and respected him. He called Tecumseh "one of those uncommon geniuses" who, had he been born anywhere but America, could have been "a founder of an empire....No difficulties deter him." That was the man Harrison was competing against.

In the summer of 1811, Harrison and Tecumseh held a series of rancorous meetings in Vincennes. The drumbeats of war were echoing. A series of Indian "massacres" of family homesteads had the frontier on a knife's edge. Reports of Native Americans massing in Prophetstown near present-day Fort Wayne deeply worried Harrison. On the other side, Tecumseh and others worried that an expedition would be mounted by the Americans to destroy his confederacy. The Vincennes meetings did little but exacerbate the fears and suspicions on both sides. Hoping that armed conflict would not soon erupt, Tecumseh left on a trip south to try to strengthen his confederacy by adding southern tribes.

Harrison had been itching to build a fort closer to the trouble spots in northern Indiana for some time but was denied by the secretary of war, who feared it would only make matters worse. Finally, Harrison was given permission to build a fort at the northern edge of the limit of the 1809 treaty cession. That was in the area of the future Terre Haute.

Taking an army of U.S. dragoons and militia with him, Harrison had Fort Harrison built along the Wabash River in October 1811. The fort was

Later drawing of Fort Harrison. *Vigo County Historical Society.*

150 feet square with blockhouses on the west (river) side and bastions (which project out from fort walls to allow for maximum defensive fire) on the east side. The barracks were little more than crude log cabins. The fort was finished by the end of October, and then Harrison looked north.

Alarmed by news of increasing numbers of Indians massing at Prophetstown, he decided to make a preemptive strike before even more tribes of Tecumseh's confederacy joined them. Harrison and his one-thousand-strong army had settled in the high ground above Prophetstown by November 5. The troops spent a restless night on the cold, wet field. Before dawn could break, the heavily outnumbered Native American warriors attacked the militia encampment. The forces battled for two hours before the Native American attackers withdrew and abandoned Prophetstown. Harrison claimed a major victory, but at best the Battle of Tippecanoe was a draw. Harrison and the troops returned to Vincennes via Fort Harrison. The frontier remained a tinderbox. Then came a war.

The War of 1812 began in June 1812. Tecumseh and others in his confederacy immediately became allied with the British, and the center of action shifted to the north. However, one of the new war's first land battles was at Fort Harrison. The fort was then commanded by future president Captain Zachary Taylor. Bands of warriors still made forays in Indiana and Illinois territories, and news of the massacres spread alarm. Settlers had begun working the land near the fort. It made them feel less vulnerable to Indian attacks knowing that the fort and its troops were nearby. For two farmers cutting hay, that safety zone did not even extend to four hundred yards from the fort. They were set upon by a scouting party and killed on the evening of September 3, 1812.

Taylor and his command heard the sounds of the murders, but not knowing the strength of his enemy, the captain decided to wait for daylight to venture out and bury the bodies. (Years later, they were reinterred at the Porter farm north of Terre Haute.) The garrison was put on high alert. A friendly Miami had warned Taylor that an attack on the fort was being planned. A Kickapoo chief with forty or fifty warriors appeared at the fort's gate in the afternoon. He requested a meeting with Taylor the next morning. The request was likely a ruse by the Kickapoos, hoping that Taylor would assume that an attack was not imminent. The troops went about their duties, which included drawing water from the river because the well inside the fort had dried up. The troopers and nine women and children settled in for a wary night of sleep.

After dark (the reported time of the attack varies from 9:00 p.m. to 1:00 a.m. depending on which witness account is consulted), a stealthy warrior crept up to the fort from the west and set fire to a blockhouse. That was the signal for as many as six hundred warriors to fall upon the fort. Taylor rallied his men, but more than half of the troops were suffering from malaria and less than a dozen soldiers were fully fit for battle. The troopers rushed to their posts to return fire.

The situation worsened when barrels of whiskey stored in the block house caught fire and spread the blaze. A bucket brigade was started by some of the soldiers and women and children, but the water brought from the river quickly ran out. The situation was only getting worse. In desperation, they checked the well again. According to later reports, young Julia Dickson, daughter of a soldier, was lowered into the well. She discovered that the open well had refilled. Buckets were lowered and then pulled back up to douse the fires.

The battle continued throughout the night. Temporary barricades were set up behind the breaches in the fort walls caused by the fires. But the fires also illuminated the ground around the fort, allowing soldiers to see their attackers. They began scoring hits on the warriors, all the while seven-year-old Hannah Dickson and her sisters carried guns back and forth to their mother to be reloaded and returned to the soldiers on the firing line.

The battle lasted until dawn. The attackers were losing more and more warriors, and their ammunition was running perilously low. They withdrew. Thus began the siege of Fort Harrison. The Native American band decided to see if they could "wait out" the defenders until they were starving and would perhaps surrender.

Their only concession to the fort was allowing the women to go to the river to draw water, as the well had once again gone dry. It was a tense week before reinforcements arrived, and the siege broke on the twelfth. The Native American force slipped away. The battle became the source of many tales over the years. Hannah (Dickson) Burnett was the last survivor. Shortly before her death, she told a story of that night. She claimed that during the battle, the face of a warrior was illuminated, and she saw what she called a "blab," a silver ornament, in his nose. The next day, she said, her father ventured out of the fort and found that warrior dead. He cut the blab from his nose and gave it her as a memento of the battle.

The Battle of Fort Harrison is considered the first land victory of the War of 1812 for the Americans by some historians. But the war continued to the north. Tecumseh and the confederacy and their British allies initially had some success. But Tecumseh and his dream died when he was killed and his forces routed at the Battle of the Thames in Canada in October 1813.

CAMP HARRISON PRISONER OF WAR CAMP

The Battle of Fort Donelson made General Ulysses S. Grant's reputation as an aggressive warrior. From February 11 to February 16, 1862, Grant, on his own initiative, pushed his troops across the rain-sodden fields of northern Tennessee. With the help of a Union gunboat squadron, Grant's army forced the surrender of Confederate troops. When Confederate commanders asked for terms of their capitulation, Grant coolly replied his only acceptable terms were "unconditional and immediate surrender."

Thus, Grant gained a nickname—"Unconditional Surrender" Grant—and, more problematically, more than six thousand prisoners of war. The dispirited prisoners—many of them ill, weak and underfed—were loaded on steamboats and sent north on the Mississippi River.

The unexpected number of prisoners overwhelmed Union capabilities, and states were asked to take on a share of the burden. Indiana's vaunted wartime governor, Oliver Morton, quickly agreed to help, and a major POW camp was set up on the Indianapolis fairgrounds called, naturally, Camp Morton. But that was not enough, and the governor asked other cities to set up camps. Terre Haute quickly agreed to host a camp.

The new "prison" in Terre Haute was in the unused Farrington & Williams pork packinghouse. The large building was located hard by the Wabash River at First and Park Streets (present-day Fairbanks Park). Colonel B.F. Morton of the Sixty-First (Irish) Regiment was appointed commander of the site, called Camp Harrison.

The first trainload of prisoners headed for Camp Morton passed through Terre Haute on the morning of February 22. A crowd of curious Hauteans watched the train pass through and wondered when "their" POWs would arrive. Four days later, they had their answer.

A trainload of prisoners chugged into the Terre Haute station at 1:00 a.m. on February 26. The POWs were held in the train cars until daybreak. Around 8:00 a.m., Colonel Mullen and his detachment of guards arrived to escort the prisoners to their new home. From the cramped train cars emerged a ragged group of weary Confederate soldiers. They trudged a few blocks past curious onlookers to their new home.

After the prisoners were marched into the camp, Mullen had them searched. The guards then received a great shock: they found their charges still armed! Many of the POWs still had knives, handguns and ammunition on them. It could have been a disaster, but they quietly handed over their weapons. Mullen was shocked at the "want of care" by the army when the prisoners were loaded onto the boats in Tennessee or offloaded in Cairo, Illinois, and not checked for arms. Still, he said, the prisoners were "tractable and orderly." It also shows that the prisoners had had their guts-full of war and did not even attempt to rise up and escape. For them, their war was over, and they seemed relieved at that.

Historians have debated for years over relative merits of POW camps in the North versus the often-squalid Confederate camps. The infamy of the horrible conditions for Union POWs at the notorious Andersonville prison camp in Georgia was held as the dubious exemplar of Southern camps. However, it was found that many Northern POW camps were not as well run as previously thought. There were Northern camps where prisoners were kept in unsanitary conditions, fed poor food and lacked medical care. Two of the worst Northern camp were at Elmira, New York (called "Hellmira" by its POWs), and Camp Douglas in Chicago. Nearly four thousand Confederate soldiers died at Camp Douglas. Even Camp Morton, which was often held up as a good example of a well-run camp, was called into dispute when a Confederate prisoner's memoir of his time there was published in a national magazine more than twenty-five years after the war and caused a national debate.

By all accounts, Camp Harrison was well run during its brief six-month existence. The prisoners received the same rations as their guards, and attempts were made to make the pork packinghouse turned prison as sanitary as possible. One interesting aspect of camp life was the reaction of Terre Haute's citizens. Most seemed to have felt a genuine sympathy for the POWs. Apparently, they were not seen merely as the enemy. Colonel Mullen asked that a notice be placed in Indianapolis newspapers thanking Terre Haute's citizens for their generosity. He noted that many donated covers and quilts to help keep the prisoners warm during the bad weather. They also donated books, periodicals and writing paper to help ease the prisoners' plight. Mullen gave any minister in town who wished them twenty-five passes to visit the camp and conduct Sunday services. They were eagerly accepted.

However, Camp Harrison suffered from the same problem as any other camp: disease. Prisoners often arrived at camps weakened, and many were already plagued by disease, sometimes leading to epidemics. Typhoid fever broke out at Camp Harrison and led to the establishment of Terre Haute's first hospital. A "makeshift" hospital was set up near the prison in mid-March. A local physician named Rust was placed in charge of the hospital, and nursing staff was provided by the Sisters of Providence. Rust was joined by other local doctors to oversee patient care.

Again the locals donated to the hospital, and so many tried to visit the hospital that Indiana's Adjutant General Noble had to issue a set of regulations governing it. Among the regulations were that any donations had to be shared equally among all patients, only underclothing donations were permitted and only visitors of proven loyalty to the Union were permitted to enter the wards. Taking advantage of the situation, a local merchant advertised for seamstresses to sew 350 bed sacks, 350 pillow cases and 700 hospital sheets.

The hospital obviously provided great care and helped stop what could have been the rapid spread of typhoid fever. Of the nearly seven hundred prisoners in the camp, only eleven died—one from pneumonia. In addition, one guard succumbed to typhoid fever. The death rate from disease was much lower than at other camps. One of those who died was George Zollicoffer of the Ninth Tennessee. He was the half brother of former congressman Felix Zollicoffer, who was a brigadier general in the Confederate army. The general was killed at the Battle of Mill Springs just two weeks prior to his brother's capture. The soldiers were buried in the potters' field section of Woodlawn Cemetery. After the war, a monument inscribed with names of the dead soldiers was erected on the cemetery grounds.

The deaths of their fellow soldiers spurred a petition to Governor Morton, signed by all but twenty-five of the prisoners, asking that they be released on an oath of loyalty so as not to contract typhoid. Two prisoners did manage to escape in late March, but it appears their hearts weren't really in it. They were caught later that day less than three miles from the camp. When asked why they did not attempt to run farther and faster, one replied, "Well, this is good country and we decided to settle."

There may have been a very curious anomaly among the prisoners. An Indianapolis paper reported that there were "contrabands" among the prisoners (contraband was the Civil War term for escaped slaves or associated with Union troops). If true, these contrabands may have been slaves who worked at Fort Donelson; it was also not unheard of for some slaves to accompany their masters into the army and continue to serve them on the battlefield. No other word about them was forthcoming.

Gradually, over the early summer, many prisoners left the camp. Some were transferred to other camps, and some may have switched sides and joined the Union forces or been "paroled." Parolees were those who swore allegiance to the Union and agreed not to rejoin the Confederate armies if allowed to return home.

No matter the reason, Camp Harrison was emptied and closed by July 1862.

The Lurking Spy

Unknown to all but a few, Terre Haute was only fifteen miles from the center of a Confederate spy ring that was operating in Marshall, Illinois, in 1864. It was a part of what is now known as the Northwest Conspiracy.

The conspiracy was a series of efforts in 1864 and 1865 to destabilize the North by committing acts of sabotage, fomenting insurrection by Confederate supporters in the North known as "Copperheads" and

"Butternuts." Ultimately, they hoped to free Confederate prisoners in the North, particularly those in Camp Douglas in Chicago and Camp Morton in Indianapolis. The POWs then could either rejoin their units in the South or remain behind as guerrillas in Union territory. The idea was the brainchild of Thomas Hines, a dashing Confederate cavalryman complete with flowing mustache. Hines had made an earlier raid into Indiana in 1863 to gauge support for what later became Morgan's Raid. Captured along with Morgan and his remaining forces, Hines had helped engineer their escape from an Ohio prison.

After pitching his conspiracy plan to Confederate leaders, Hines traveled to Canada, a refuge for Southern sympathizers and spies. Posing as a civilian, he crossed the border back into the United States to carry out his plan in 1864. One of his operatives was another soldier named John B. Castleman. Things did not go well in Chicago, and Hines's scheme failed for several reasons. Perhaps chief among them was that hoped-for support from the Butternut crowd did not materialize. This should not have surprised Hines or Castleman. Although Southern sympathizers in Indiana were quite vocal in their support for the Confederacy, they tended to go silent and fade away whenever they were actually called on to put their beliefs, and bodies, into action.

Undeterred, Hines and Castleman moved on to further plots in Illinois and Indiana. Calling himself "Clay Wilson," Castleman set up headquarters in Marshall, Illinois. He may have lodged at the Archer House Hotel in Marshall, where earlier a circuit-riding lawyer named Lincoln stayed, but most likely he was housed by sympathizers. The stretch between Terre Haute and Marshall was considered one of the most hardcore Butternut areas in the region. It was an enclave that gleefully hid deserters and those fleeing the draft. The "headquarters" was a stone house in Clark County, Illinois, along Big Creek known locally as Castle Fin. Its "commander" was a Confederate officer named Colonel James T.R. Allen, aka Pete Johnson or Powder Head #2. It was at Castle Fin that plots were hatched. Castleman began making connections with Copperheads in the area. In a report to the Confederate government, he said that Hines was operating out of Mattoon, Illinois.

Hines and Castleman's little guerrilla network did actually pull off a few acts of sabotage, including blowing up some Union storehouses. But they wanted to do more. One of their major plots was to blow up a flotilla of Union boats moored in St. Louis.

Castleman learned that the besieged city of Vicksburg was supplied by the quartermaster corps in St. Louis. If they could destroy the steamboats that carried those supplies downriver, they could disrupt the Union efforts. He sent one of his men from Marshall, George B. Eastin, to St. Louis to reconnoiter the situation. Eastin returned with a list of the steamboats and their names. Castleman and ten of his men immediately returned to St. Louis to carry out the mission. They checked separately into a hotel near the docks.

After breakfast, they headed out. Each boarded his assigned ship. There was no security in place, and locals could come and go from the boats as they wished. Looking for most combustible or easily ignited areas, they placed their incendiary devices. They returned to their rooms to await the destruction. But nothing happened. Their devices were made of "Greek fire." These incendiaries were first used in the seventh century. Believed to be made from naphtha and quicklime, Greek fire was most often used in navel battles, as it would continue to burn while floating on water. Whatever mixture Castleman and his crew concocted failed to ignite. He later said it would have been better to send his men armed with matches to set the seventy-three boats ablaze.

Castleman still wanted to lead a band of Illinois and Indiana sympathizers to attack Camp Morton and free the prisoners for their little army. On September 29, Castleman left Marshall and rode to Sullivan, Indiana. He was to meet with a group of sympathizers there organized by a man named Humphrey. He instructed others to meet him there.

Quite unknown to him, the braggadocio of some of Hines's men in Mattoon about the plans was overheard and reported to authorities. Castleman and two co-conspirators were captured. It all seemed over for the man calling himself Clay Wilson.

But Thomas Hines, who was known for daredevil escapes from danger, had other ideas. He rushed to Terre Haute with some of his men with the idea of freeing Castleman when the train taking him to prison in Indianapolis stopped at Terre Haute. Hines and his men were ready as the train chugged in from the south. As later recounted by Vigo County Historian Mike McCormick in an excellent article about the event:

> *Strategically placed around the Terre Haute Depot, Hines' spies awaited a cue to gun down the guards. Moments before the signal, a train loaded with Union soldiers chugged into the station. Castleman, flanked by sentinels, saw the infantrymen arrive. Hines did not. Attentive to the insurgents'*

John Castleman during Civil War. *Author's collection.*

> *designs, Castleman hastily requested a well-dressed man standing nearby to warn Hines to "back off." The man obliged; the warning averted a major incident in Terre Haute on September 30, 1864.*

The train carrying Castleman and his captured men steamed east to Indianapolis. No one on it but Castleman was aware how close they came to bloodshed. Castleman was charged as a spy. The complaint read that he "did secretly and covertly lurk and travel about as a spy in the dress of a civilian." He received the death sentence and was sent to prison. But Castleman, who had joined the Confederate army at age nineteen, received a stay of execution signed by President Lincoln.

After the war, Castleman was briefly exiled to France, where he studied medicine until President Andrew Johnson pardoned him in 1866. Castleman returned to Louisville and became a successful businessman. A militia unit he revived in 1878 became the First Kentucky Volunteers during the Spanish-American War. Castleman was promoted to brigadier general during the war and later served as military governor of Puerto Rico.

When Castleman joined the Confederate army, he supported slavery, but he was a man who changed much over his life. He became a strong advocate of racial justice in Louisville. He fought against lynchings and integrated Louisville's park system. However, his statue in Louisville was removed by the city in 2020.

Strikes Three

America: A Land of Interchangeable Parts

Eli Whitney, celebrated inventor of the cotton gin, is often credited with introducing the concept and practice of interchangeable parts. Working for a military armory, Whitney strove to make parts or components to identical specifications. They then could be easily assembled by almost anyone, regardless of skill. Prior to that, each gun was unique and painstakingly made by talented gunsmiths. That took time and was expensive. If one could provide interchangeable parts, in essence any pair of hands could do it. Thus, manufacturing products became easier, cheaper and more profitable. In the early twentieth century, Henry Ford married interchangeable with the assembly line, and a new industrial revolution began.

Those parts were made of metal or wood, but long before that, centuries before the birth of the United States, there had always been interchangeable parts. These parts were made of flesh and bone and called workers. If your job called more for brawn than brains, hard labor more than advanced skills, then you were merely a human interchangeable part to business owners. A coal miner killed in a slate fall or explosion could easily be replaced by another human interchangeable part. Work would continue with your replacement part. If you were a laborer on a construction site or laying track for a railroad and you fell to your death or were crushed, well, a new part would soon be seamlessly fitted into your place.

THE TERRE HAUTE STAR — FINAL EDITION

TERRE HAUTE, IND., WEDNESDAY, SEPTEMBER 6, 1922 — PRICE 3c

RAILROAD WORKER AND STRIKER ARE SHOT

SENATE CRITICISM FACES DAUGHERTY FOR STRIKE WRIT

Injunction Against Unions in Rail Walkout Held to Be Too Drastic—Reaction Unfavorable.

BY DAVID LAWRENCE.

News Summary

SEVEN NON-UNION WORKERS DIE IN BUNK HOUSE FIRE

TWO WOUNDED IN AUTO BATTLE AT LARRIMER HILL

Strikers in Car Open Fire on Machine Bearing Shop Workers—One Non-Union Man Expected to Die.

DAUGHERTY SAYS PERSONAL RIGHTS

BISHOP FALLOWS DIES AFTER SHORT ILLNESS

ANOTHER WOMAN IS HUNTED AT IN

EDUCATOR ATTACKS LEGISLATIVE CRAZE

Author's collection.

And if you did die or lost an arm or leg, good luck to your family. They might be offered a pittance in compensation (how much was that guy's leg worth, again?). Then again, they might not. From 1890 to 1920, in particular, seldom a week went by without a story, or stories, about industrial accidents, usually followed by notices of the families of the victims having to sue owners to get some sort of compensation. The worth of that human part was then calculated. The story of the Larimer Hill Shootout is an example.

The Railway Shopmen's strike of 1922 spread across the nation, ultimately involving more than 400,000 railroad workers. It was the largest strike against the incredibly powerful railroad owners since the great Pullman Strike of 1894. It was the outgrowth of railroad workers' growing anger about wage cuts following World War I (during which the government nationalized the country's railroads). In addition, railroad owners increasingly "hired" outside "contractors" to circumvent legally negotiated labor contracts and their provisions that protected the workers' rights. The final blow was the owners demanding a second pay cut in less than two years. That pay cut of seven cents per hour may seem paltry today, but in 1922 it meant a loss of 12 percent of the workers' income. And, said the owners, if they don't like it we can always replace them.

So, the shopmen called a strike. Shopmen were the boilermakers, machinists and laborers who maintained the rolling stock of railroads. They were the men who kept the rails humming. A union report after the strike summed up the workers' view:

> *Brotherhood leadership had hoped to hold fast to standards of wages, hours and working conditions as stipulated in the National Agreement, in a belief that somewhat decreased living costs would result in that agreement providing fair remuneration. But the first wage reduction was followed by a decision on August 11, 1921, dealing with overtime, eliminating time-and-one-half for Sunday and holiday work and modifying other sections of the overtime agreements.*
>
> *The effect of this decision was electrifying. To the Brotherhood membership it was a piecemeal decision on one part of the National Agreement indicating what was to come as other decisions were handed down. Moreover, these actions in Washington were directly responsible for an increasingly hostile attitude toward workers on the part of railroad management, particularly local subordinates, who appeared to adopt a manner of treatment calculated to stir the workers to drastic action.*

The Pennsy Yard in Terre Haute was one of the largest repair sites in the country at the time. The workers there joined in the strike on June 30, 1922. The management decided that it could then replace the union workers with non-union men. After all, they would work cheaper and did not have the benefits prescribed for the union workers under their contract.

This use of "replacement workers" was an insidious part of management's treatment of workers. Management knew that interchangeable human parts were available and eager for work. In effect, this was setting worker against worker. There were always men who would be "scabs," the accepted term in those days—others might say "strikebreakers." But strikebreakers were really those who were brought in the physically break the strikers. Owners hired private armies of desperate men who thuggishly arrived on the scene to break a few strikers' heads or backs or knees.

But often owners did not have to resort to that. The government, particularly state governors, feared strikes. Often beholden to owners for their political support and fearful of damaging the economy, governors would call out the state militia, supposedly to maintain order. Often the militia's guns were turned on the strikers.

So the Pennsy Yard began to hire scabs. Many men were eager to hire on. Frank Easterday was a thirty-year-old from Marshall, Illinois, with a wife and young son to support. He had spent most of his life as a farm laborer around Clark County. He knew there might be difficulties taking a job at the yard, but working for the railroad was a coveted job. He hired on.

Easterday drove the twenty miles to Terre Haute along the National Road with fellow laborers, including Ralph Beabout and Russel Hill. They could share expenses and did not have to travel alone. If trouble happened, you always felt a bit safer to have friends with you—and if you carried a little protection under the seat so much the better. Each day as they drove into the huge railyard they faced a picket of strikers. Jeers were shouted; perhaps stones or decaying vegetables were tossed at their car. It was an intimidating scene to start and end the workday. But it was worth it to Easterday to have a steady job that paid more than working on a farm.

Seeing the scabs take their jobs infuriated the strikers. During long days on the picket line, the strikers talked angrily among themselves. Those scabs were taking food out of their families' mouths. Bastards. Something should be done about them. They were as bad as the big shots who ran the railroad.

On Tuesday, September 5, Easterday and his buddies hurried to their car at the end of their shift. Another day of work over; they just wanted to go home. They headed south to Wabash Avenue to head home to Marshall.

As Easterday drove out of the yard, five strikers in two cars watched them leave—let's follow the bastards, put a scare in the sons of bitches, they thought. In the lead strikers' car were Lawrence Huffman, Herman Clugston and George Huebel. They tailed Easterday's car until they reached Fourteenth and Wabash, where they passed it. They knew where he lived and the route he would take home. They kept just ahead of Easterday's car as they drove west on Wabash Avenue and crossed the bridge. At the end of the grade east of West Terre Haute, the strikers slowed down and let Easterday pass them. They wound slowly along National Avenue.

Seeing the strikers' car, Easterday, who must have been suspicious, now had his fears realized. Leaving West Terre Haute, he hit the accelerator, pushing his car up Larimer Hill. Seeing that, Huffman also sped up. The cars were abreast as they neared the top of the hill. Shots rang out from both cars. The cars veered off the road during the mayhem. Residents reported that they heard at least ten shots. It was like a shootout from the movies.

It was over in minutes. Two strikers, Huffman and Clugston, were slightly wounded. Three bullets pierced Easterday's side and legs. Blood filled the front seat. His buddies, who were uninjured, watched in horror. The strikers fled, running through a field to reach the tile plant outside West Terre Haute. Huffman and Clugston stopped there to get a drink of water and await the police.

Ambulances arrived. Easterday was immediately taken back across the grade to St. Anthony's Hospital. It did not look good. Huffman was taken to Dr. Kunkler's office in West Terre Haute, where the good doctor dressed his wound. Clugston was taken to Terre Haute and fixed up; he then went to one of his haunts, a pool room at Fifteenth and Locust. It was there he was later arrested.

One of Easterday's companions drove his car home to Marshall after talking to the police. Easterday's wife, Cora, and five-year-old Eugene were waiting for Frank to get home. When the car finally pulled up to their rented house and their husband and father did not step out as usual, their world changed. Frank Easterday died the following day.

Six strikers were charged with murder after Easterday's death. Easterday's companions were charged with shooting with intent to kill. Ultimately, with both sides saying that the other started the shootout, the Vigo Circuit Court did not bring in indictments. All eleven were set free. The railroad, which had pushed hard for the strikers to be tried and convicted of murder, got a little bit of revenge afterward. It pushed for a federal judge to charge Huffman, Clugston and the others for violating a court order stipulating that strikers could not harass the replacement workers. They spent a few weeks in jail in Indianapolis.

There is no evidence that any of the strikers returned to the railroad shop where they once worked. They found other jobs. They weren't missed by the railroad. Like the dead Frank Easterday, who was one of eleven people nationwide to die in the strike, it was easy to find replacement parts.

SIEGE OF DIXIE BEE MINE

The year 1932 was a bad time in the Indiana coal fields. The Great Depression was an eviscerating cancer loose throughout the land. Mines were closing. The owners of those still open were trying to squeeze every penny from the buried black diamonds by trying to make union miners work for less than union scale or bringing in non-union crews who would work for much less. It was pitting hardworking men against other hard workers—

men who might once have seen one another as brothers now saw people who wanted to take away their livelihoods. Those who were once allies now only saw enemies. That happened at the Dixie Bee Mine, a deep-shaft mine just south of Terre Haute.

The union miners at Dixie Bee fought hard to maintain their union-scale jobs of $6.10 per day. In February 1932, they filed a petition to dissolve the lease held by a Chicago man. He had subleased the mine to a cooperative mine group. Cooperative mine corporations were usually small groups that leased mines. Sometimes these groups were made up of both owners and miners. The co-op group was paying less than the scale stipulated by the lease. Nothing came of their petition because the contract between the United Mine Workers of America ended on March 31. With no binding contract, owners could drive down wages, and there was nothing union miners could do about it.

Like other owners, the Dixie Bee group dropped wages to four dollars per day, or even lower. They hired non-union men who were desperate for work, no matter their wage. Union miners began picketing Dixie Bee. So hungry were they that some picketers hoped to be arrested because they knew they would be fed in jail. The first physical confrontation took place in early April. Nearly five hundred picketers gathered on the road leading to the mine in an attempt to stop non-union miners from entering the mine. When some refused to honor the picket line, they were pulled from their cars, and eleven men were "beaten and cut" and their car windows smashed. Such confrontations were ongoing.

By July, the owners had guards and a machine gun mounted on the coal tipple. Tensions rose steadily. One owner told authorities, "Everybody is on edge. A serious conflict may break out at any moment." He was right.

On July 28, more than one thousand protestors surrounded the mine at dawn. They refused to allow seventeen night shift miners to leave and turned away one hundred men who arrived for their day shifts. It was getting ugly. Vigo County sheriff Joe Dreher and a small band of deputies tried to maintain peace. Dreher knew how explosive the situation had become, and he and city officials sent the first of their appeals to Indiana governor Henry Leslie for additional help.

The number of picketers had grown to an estimated three thousand by the next day. The situation was getting out of hand. There were armed guards inside the mine site, angry protesters outside and fewer than ten deputies to try to control things. But most of the picketers left for the weekend after hearing that the governor was going to try to mediate between the sides. However, nothing was resolved.

Dixie Bee reopened on Monday, August 1. One hundred non-union miners moved warily through the gates and headed to the shaft. Picketers began to arrive in force. Dreher sent his second request for help to the governor. The siege of Dixie Bee Mine had begun.

More and more picketers arrive. By Tuesday afternoon, the protesters had swelled to at least three thousand. Other estimates said it might be six thousand protestors, many from out of state. Authorities would later claim that the proverbial "outside agitators" were to blame. Crowds of onlookers also milled around to see for themselves what was happening.

The nearly one hundred miners were hoisted up from the shaft. There were fears that the picketers would rush the fan house and disable the fans that circulated air into the shaft. They were no longer miners, but defenders of a besieged garrison. Rifles and shotguns were handed out. Machine guns were cleaned and oiled, ready for a fight. There was no food at the mine, and lunches packed for the previous day's work were long gone. There was no running water. Each miner was nervous or scared or both. Who knew what might happen?

The battle began at about two o'clock in the afternoon. Both sides claimed that the other shot first. No matter who pulled the first trigger, the bullets whizzed everywhere. Two of the miners were the first to fall as bullets ripped into their bodies. There was a scramble for cover. One miner said that his hat was literally shot off his head.

Protestor Taylor Kellar of Linton, Indiana, was about to take aim when he was hit and fell to the ground. He died soon after on his way to the Sullivan hospital. The battle raged for about forty-five minutes. In the end, the losses on both sides were one dead and nine wounded (one of which was a bystander there to gawk at the protest). There were incidences of sporadic firing throughout the rest of Tuesday and the next day.

The Battle of Dixie Bee Mine finally prompted Governor Leslie to intervene. In response to the third call for help from Terre Haute officials, he announced on Wednesday morning that the area around the mine was to be placed under martial law, and he was sending in nearly one thousand National Guard troops. "I cannot permit this Guerilla warfare to continue in our state," he said in a press release. Meanwhile, the siege continued. Picketers even refused to let ambulances pass into the mine to take the wounded miners to the hospital. Inside the mine, sixty-four men (during the night as many as fifteen miners managed to slip away) and one woman, Selma Thompson, who was the wife of the mine boss, faced another day without food or water.

By then, Dixie Bee had become a front-page story on hundreds of newspapers across the country. A United Press reporter rented an airplane to fly over the scene. He reported seeing "black muzzles of guns protruding from the fan house…and tipple." He noted the picketers "changing guard with almost military precision," while others hid themselves in cornfields and boxcars. This should not have been a surprise, as undoubtedly many of the men had served in World War I.

National Guard planes flew over the site in the afternoon. Initially, they were ordered to drop tear gas canisters, but that was wisely rescinded. Protesters took potshots at the planes. For many, the arrival of the planes was a sign that things were about to change. Many decided to leave.

There were still sporadic bursts of gunfire throughout the day and evening. It was nearly midnight when 250 guardsmen arrived on the scene. Protesters continued to occasionally fire until the troops were within five hundred yards. When the bugle sounded, it was a signal of relief for the besieged miners and a cue for the protesters to melt away. The siege was over.

The freed miners eagerly told their stories. Mack Hauck, at seventy-three the oldest miner, said he lived on a chaw of tobacco for forty-one hours. Another said that he felt all rusty from all the water he drank from the boiler. Selma Thompson told three different stories about how she came to be among the besieged. First, she said she had snuck over to the mine from her house, which was only a hundred yards from the mine, on Monday. Next she said that when the firing started Tuesday afternoon, bullets were whizzing through her windows, and she braved gunfire to get to the mine. Finally, she told of her daring rescue by a miner who ran to her house, flung her over his back and ran to the mine, dodging bullets the whole way.

An anonymous miner gleefully claimed that he was the one who killed Taylor Kellar. "I saw Kellar sniping at us from a cornfield about a 100 yards away. He was trying to pick us off. I took a high-powered rifle and fired at him. I know I got him alright and he deserved it."

The siege was over. A skeleton crew of guardsmen remained in the area until October. The Dixie Bee Mine went out of business in 1933.

As a footnote to the story, a miner named Bedwell who was shot in the arm during the siege applied for workers' compensation. The Dixie Bee Mining Corporation protested his claim. The Industrial Board denied the claim, saying that his injuries "were not the result of an accident sustained by the plaintiff while in the course of his employment, nor did they arise out of his employment." Bedwell, of course, appealed this ridiculous ruling to the Indiana Court of Appeals in 1934. It did not take the court long to overturn the ruling and require that Bedwell receive his much-deserved compensation.

GENERAL STRIKE

So, you wake up in Terre Haute on Monday, July 22, 1935. You pour a cup of coffee and plan out your day. You decide that you'll hop a bus to downtown, do some shopping, grab a quick lunch and maybe catch a movie before taking the bus back home. Well, it was not going to happen, as Terre Haute was in the throes of only the third general strike in American history.

The strike was the culmination of years of labor/management conflict in the union town of Terre Haute. The year 1935 began with a strike by workers at the Stahl-Urban clothing company who wished to unionize. Those pushing for the union were fired, and a strike was called. The garment workers union continued to organize the plant workers, and after a five-week strike, the union was reluctantly recognized by management. The union victory only hardened the lines between workers and management.

Then came the Columbian Enameling and Stamping Company strike. Located on the northside, the company made enamel-coated metalware, and its relationship with its workers was often adversarial. Union workers at Columbian wanted it to be a closed shop, meaning all workers had to be unionized. Many thought the company's fondest desire was to break the union. Eliminating the union would allow the company to "do as it damn well pleased" with its workforce.

Union workers felt that non-union employees were given preferential treatment. They pointed out that company-sponsored athletic teams were composed only of non-union workers. Team members were given sweaters and team dinners provided by management. More importantly, non-union staff were given the best jobs. It was the final straw. A strike was called on March 23, 1935—450 of 485 union members walked off the job, while 35 stayed to keep the power plant working.

Picket lines were a daily presence for months. Crowds of union sympathizers joined the strikers, and there were often hundreds of people surrounding the plant. Company officials took a hard line, saying they would close the plant and would only reopen as a non-union business. Several efforts at mediation failed, as the company would not budge from its anti-union stance. The strike continued.

The strike was peaceful, with strikers and police guards fraternizing daily, even playing cards together. That changed on Saturday, July 15, when gun-toting uniformed guards entered the plant. Pro-union crowds gathered in response. The ugly mood spurred some to start throwing rocks to break plant windows. Police arrived to quiet the situation. After midnight, more stones

Protesters gather outside Columbian Enameling. *Vigo County Historical Society.*

flew through the air. Union picketers claimed that the guards instigated the rock throwing to incite the crowd. If so, it worked.

Some of the crowd broke into the plant office. They found boxes of bullets stored there and began tossing them out windows, which only incited the crowd. Sensing the crowd's mood, the guards who had been hired to protect the plant ran and hid. Police returned on Sunday morning to escort the guards out to protect them from the crowds. Union officials said they could not control the outside supporters and took out a newspaper ad saying that no union members were involved in storming the plant. Additionally, they were placing twenty-four union members to guard the plant.

Further efforts at mediation were useless. The chamber of commerce hosted a meeting of city officials and business owners that firmly came down against the strikers. Battle lines were drawn.

Saying that they feared further violence, the company brought in fifty extra "guards" from Chicago on July 18. The guards, union members protested, were nothing but union-busting thugs. They asked the city to prevent the importation of the guards. Instead, city police met the bus carrying them at Memorial Stadium, swore them in as special deputies and escorted them to the plant. Armed with submachine guns and shotguns, the "guards" patrolled the plant.

Labor was incensed by the owners' latest move. The next day, a meeting was convened in which participants of nearly fifty unions attended. Three thousand union supporters later gathered at the courthouse to protest the use of guards. They voted to initiate a general strike unless the strikebreakers were sent back to Chicago. That did not happen.

A shopkeeper closes store to honor the general strike. *Author's collection.*

An estimated 90 percent of businesses took part in the strike, including filling stations, barbershops and even taverns. Workers at Terre Haute Malleable, Western Fiber Box and Hulman Company joined the strike, as did employees of two meatpacking plants and eight coal mines. Strikers fanned out through the city to "encourage" businesses that remained open to join the cause. Business owners who hesitated received an obscenity-filled tongue lashing and broken windows. Not all were intimidated. A Mrs. J. Moore who owned a small neighborhood grocery met the strikers at her door with a .32 revolver and a promise to offer trouble for trouble. By Tuesday, she had to hire extra clerks to serve customers who rushed to buy groceries.

Panicked Terre Haute officials, saying they feared mob violence, telegrammed Indiana governor Paul McNutt on Monday for help. McNutt responded by declaring martial law for Vigo County for the second time in three years. By Monday evening, 1,100 Indiana National Guardsmen and officers had arrived in Terre Haute; 600 guardsman were quickly dispatched to Columbian Enameling. About 2,000 protesters crowded into the neighborhood Tuesday morning. They attempted to prevent the soldiers from entering the plant but were pushed back. Terre Haute police then launched tear gas into the crowd. The protesters reluctantly dispersed.

The troops then set up machine gun nests in the plant and sent out armed sentries to enforce a two-block cordon around the plant. Some of the protesters emerged from alleys and streets Tuesday afternoon to continue their protests. Rocks once again became missiles. One hit its target, breaking two ribs of a guardsmen. Tear gas was once again fired, and one hundred protesters were arrested. Heavy rains dampened the ardor of many protesters.

Two Department of Labor officials arrived in town to calm the situation. They announced that talks between the two parties would be arranged. A union leader went on the radio Tuesday night to say that the general strike was called off. The news only angered the remaining protesters at the plant. For the fourth time that day, tear gas was used to disperse them. Relative calm then prevailed.

The National Guard provided escorts into the plant for non-union workers when they restarted production. The hired guards were no longer needed and were sent packing, but not before four of them made their presence felt. The four smuggled out a few tear gas canisters and proceeded to the notorious red-light district in the west end. They caused "considerable disorder" along the brothel-lined streets before police arrested them.

National Guard on duty in Terre Haute. *Vigo County Historical Society.*

The general strike was lifted. Luckily, the disorders led to only three injuries—two Guardsmen were injured by rocks and a female protester cut her hand on a Guardsman's bayonet as she attempted to enter the plant. Terre Haute cooled down, but each side warily eyed the other. A group calling itself the Law and Order League was formed in response to the strikers. Saying that they were opposed to "violence and mob rule," they employed World War I veterans (paying them one dollar per day) to act as an unofficial police force. A professor at Indiana State viewed the league as an attempt to bring fascism to Terre Haute. They were never used.

Martial law continued. Norman Thomas, the 1932 presidential candidate of the Socialist Party of America, decried the use of martial law in an article published in the liberal magazine *The Nation*. Titled "Hoosier Hitlerism," Thomas called it a perniciously effective denial of civil rights used by "that handsome Hoosier Hitler, Governor Paul McNutt." He went on to say that the "strong arm of federal government [and state and local governments] has been effectively extended time and time again for the protection of property. Seldom has it been used to protect life and liberty."

In Terre Haute, as in most other places, the governmental response to the strike was to invariably side with business interests, at least initially. In essence, it was a form of corporatism, a partnership of government and business.

Martial law continued, with a skeleton force of Guardsmen, until February 1936, but not before National Guard commander Major Earl Weimer and two of his men made fools of themselves. When refused service at a local tavern (whether because they were Guardsman or already drunk), they drew their revolvers, grabbed drinks and ordered the tavern closed.

The guardsman injured by rock heads to the hospital. *Vigo County Historical Society.*

As martial law was winding down, the union seemed to be victorious. The Regional Labor Board ruled that Columbian had committed an unfair labor practice and must "re-hire striking employees and bargain with the union." But then a federal court overturned the ruling, saying the strike violated a no-strike provision in its contract. In effect, the union had no right to act as bargaining agent for the workers. The ruling was later upheld by the Supreme Court. In the end, Columbian Enameling won. It had broken the troublesome union.

A Terre Haute Miscellany

The Teacher and the Suffragette

"A boy is capital that must be invested. A girl is of vastly less importance."

Those are the words of Bertha Pratt King from her book *A Girl's Worth*. They sum up what King fought against for most of her life. They are the reason she founded a school, became an ardent suffragist and traveled the country trying to raise the status of girls and women.

King was born in Little Falls, New York, in 1879, the daughter of a wealthy woolen mill owner. She was educated at Smith College and taught at private and public schools in the East before heading west. While visiting Terre Haute, she discovered that there were no schools preparing girls for college. With that in mind, she opened the King (originally King-Crawford) Classical School in 1907. Initially, the school was only meant for girls, but it later became coed.

The school eventually comprised three departments: high school (academic and college prep divisions) intermediate and primary. Classes were from 8:30 a.m. to 2:00 p.m. The early dismissal allowed students outdoor recreation during the "best part of the day." The stature of the school grew steadily, and within ten years, it had been certified by schools like Michigan, Nebraska, Wellesley and Smith, which stipulated that graduates of King Classical were automatically accepted without entrance exams.

Left: Bertha Pratt King. *Vigo County Historical Society*.

Below: King Classical School. *Vigo County Historical Society*.

King was an early and strong proponent of what is known today as STEM learning. Both the academic and college prep classes included physics, plane geometry, biology and chemistry requirements. This was part of her belief that girls must work to overcome the conventions of the time that said women were unsuited to the nature of scientific pursuits. Her aspiration was to instill in her students "a desire for knowledge and develop control and personal responsibility." Many of her students said she "opened vistas of thought that they never thought existed."

Not surprisingly, King was an active suffragette. She toured the Midwest, organizing and speaking to suffragette groups. Her most difficult area was northern Ohio. She later recalled the bad old days when women stumping for the vote were spat on, egged and thrown out of meetings.

She also organized a suffrage club for girls under fifteen called the Juvenile Equal Franchise League. It was for the girl who "wishes to be identified with this movement for the emancipation of women from the narrowing conventions under which have been living under." As a paper noted, such efforts were the reason "the conservative element [in Terre Haute] shakes its head" about what they viewed as King's radical views. The paper defended her by saying that the reaction to her on the causes of women and their economic and sociological concerns were to King's credit. It showed her strength and aspirations for a better world.

In 1914, King was asked to join the Redpath Chautauqua circuit. That began a second career for her. Thereafter, she would spend time traveling around the country, discussing the social and cultural issues confronting women. A much sought-after speaker, she also delivered addresses on the lives of famous women throughout history.

King did not marry until she was sixty-six years old. She married seventy-three-year-old Terre Haute poet Max Ehrmann in 1945. The poet's most famous work was *Desiderata* ("Go placidly amid the noise and haste…"), which became something of an anthem during the turbulent 1970s. Unfortunately, Ehrmann died three months after their marriage. It was a difficult year for King, who had to close King Classical that year due to declining enrollment. Still, she carried on as a local community leader supporting various causes.

In a decidedly sad irony when she died in 1962, obituaries spent more time talking about her husband and only later detailing her achievements. The woman who spent most of her life trying to see that women be known for who they were was overshadowed by her husband of three months.

IDA HUSTED HARPER WAS a writer. In a period when most women were expected to be docile, dull-eyed members of the Cult of Domesticity, she spoke out. Her columns in the *Terre Haute Saturday Evening Mail* were remarkably candid, enlivened by an understated humor and with more than a touch of sly sarcasm. As Harper was an ardent suffragette, a column she wrote in 1882 and the following reply "by a Woman" serve as examples of the divide over women's rights among women.

In the column, Harper wrote that everyone was glad the 1882 elections were over. "Most of all the candidates, next, the citizens and lastly, 'the women folks.'" Why the women folks, she asked? She then slyly pointed out the things that women cannot do that keep men away from home and family during elections. Women can't go and get drunk celebrating or mourning the results, can't go to ward meetings, stay out all night or vote at any rate. She noted, "One politician in a family can demoralize a family."

She noted that the election was only a choice of two evils and offered a sly dig at the results. "Well, let us be thankful. People wanted a change. They said the Republicans were getting too fat at their expense and so they turned in the starving Democrats to eat up what little the Republicans had left." She closed by saying if women get the vote, the whole election system will have to change and expand—places other than saloons, stables and alleyways must be added to voting locations.

"A Woman" replied one month later in the same paper. She seemed upset that Harper and other women's rights advocates used any report of a woman in an unusual occupation to push for suffrage or other rights. After pointing out that there are two sides to every story, she then listed her objections to Harper's article. She began her objections with the quite unoriginal "just because," followed by the "you can catch more flies with honey than vinegar" analogy. This was driven by the author's perception that suffragettes held strong feelings against men. The more effective way to get what they wanted was to show their strength by cooking a good dinner. A nice meal waiting on the table will cause him to say, "After all these strong-minded women are not as bad as they are represented." In other words, Susan B. Anthony would be more successful in her efforts if she stayed quiet, put a good pot roast on the table and let men decide if they wanted to support a woman's right to vote than make a strident speech.

The author then wrote of free speech. Suffragettes can say what they want, but she thought their harping on about female superiority over men was not supported by facts. Women's rights advocates were ungrateful for not realizing how good they had it in America. "American gentlemen," she wrote, "are nature's noblemen." Worse, such women were unpatriotic because they resorted to "arraying the sexes against each other" and ungodly because their views went against "family life as God intended."

Born in Franklin, Indiana, Ida Husted Harper arrived in Terre Haute as a very young bride of nineteen or twenty. Her husband, Thomas Harper, was a lawyer. She later spoke of being "very lonely" in Terre Haute. She came to have very strong, not-so-loving feelings about her adopted hometown. "There is not a city of its size any place where education, refinement and true worth count for so little and wealth and display so much." The best she could later say about her fellow Hauteans was, "Terre Haute society can dance and can dress. Let us claim that much for them and then stay silent."

Harper's writing career was unexpected. It began when she wrote letters to the editor about pieces in the paper with which she disagreed. Her ideas and writing talent intrigued the editor of the *Saturday Evening Mail.* He hired her to write for the paper. At first, she did not receive a byline. Eventually, she wrote under the pseudonym Mrs. John Smith. After she was "outed," she wrote under her own name, signing herself Ida A. Harper. Her column, "A Woman's Opinion," ran for a dozen years. As noted, she was not averse to sharing opinions that flew in the face of conventional wisdom.

An Indianapolis newspaper took note of Harper in 1884 in a glowing article about her abilities. She "wields a bold, vigorous and incisive pen. She analyses with consumative ability. She probes with the steady hand of an experienced surgeon." It was especially impressed with her takes on politics. She wrote of "political shadows" in a way to find substance. Harper also began a column for women in Eugene V. Debs's *Brotherhood of Locomotive Engineers* magazine.

By 1880, she was a mother and secretary of the Indiana branch of the National Women's Suffrage Association. That year, she met a woman who became a friend, mentor and beacon in her life. Susan B. Anthony appeared at a three-day conference in Dowling Hall in Terre Haute. The conference was well covered, although newspaper reporters spent an inordinate time describing the physical appearances of Anthony and other female speakers. That conference changed Harper's life.

In 1890, she divorced her husband and left him and Terre Haute behind. Initially, she moved to Indianapolis to work for the cause. She eventually became the publicist for the National Women's Suffrage Association and one of the most prominent in the inner circle around Anthony. She was perhaps the suffrage icon's closest companion. She lived with Anthony while bringing

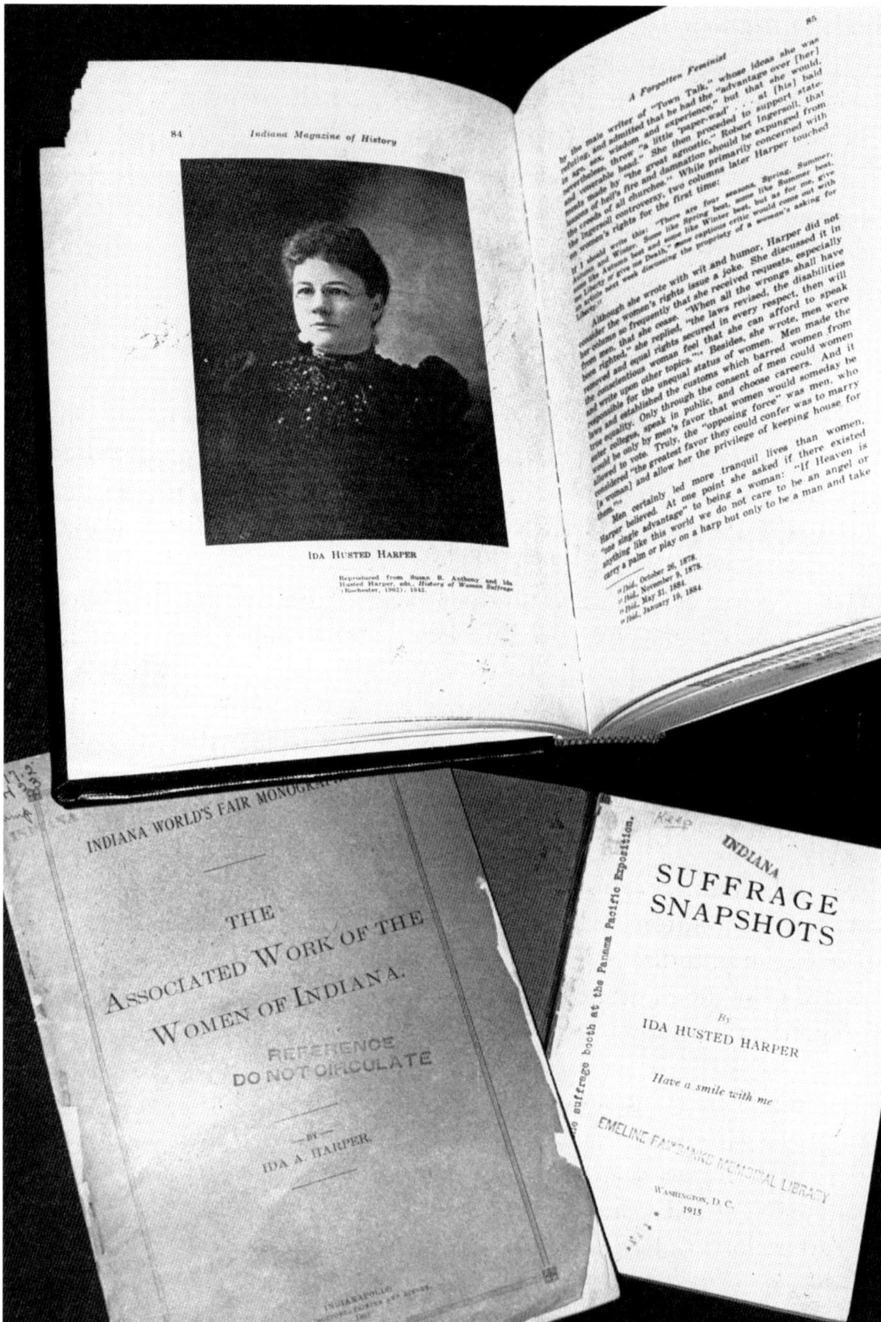

Ida Husted Harper. *Vigo County Historical Society.*

order to Anthony's papers and correspondence. Harper's most important work was her three-volume biography of Anthony.

Harper continued to champion causes after the right to vote was won and Anthony's death. In 1930, she lived in Washington, D.C., and listed her occupation as "lecturer." She died in Washington in 1931. She was buried in Delaware County, Indiana.

Pearl Divers and Ragpickers

One doesn't often associate the Wabash River with French nobility, but in the first decade of the twentieth century, they were indeed connected. Pearls from the Wabash became a must-have haute couture item in Paris. At the zenith of the fad, a Wabash River pearl had such a cachet that the best examples sold for as much as $1,500 each.

These were, of course, freshwater pearls extracted from the meat of mussels found in the river, not saltwater pearls found in oysters. Still, they were high-quality and more abundant than saltwater pearls. Mussels could contain as many as twenty to fifty pearls. Pearls were formed when an irritant like a bug or piece of grit became lodged within their shell. Oysters and mussels "treated" irritants by covering them in layers of nacre, a substance that coated the inside of the shells. Eventually, a pearl was formed. Nacre was also known as mother of pearl.

Mussels had previously been collected for their shells, which were used to make buttons or other decorative items. Exactly when the pearl craze began in Indiana is unknown, but by 1900, "pearlers" were digging mussels near the mouth of the Wabash in Vincennes. The practice then worked its way up the river. Terre Hauteans began their pearling efforts around 1904.

Some diggers focused on sandbars. They followed the jagged trails left by the mussels until they found where they had buried themselves, usually two to three inches deep under the sand. But that was a very hit-and-miss operation. The hardcore pearlers preferred the fishing method.

Pearl fishing involved two main methods: hooking and raking. Implements shaped like anchors, with multiple hooks, were dragged along the riverbeds in the hope they would grab mussels. Rake fishing featured what looked like oversized pliers. The rakes had pitchfork-looking devices on the end that could be opened and closed. After a period of dragging along the bed,

THE INDIANAPOLIS NEWS, SATURDAY, DECEMBER 5, 1908.

PEOPLE ALONG THE WABASH RIVER HAVE GONE MAD IN THEIR SEARCH FOR PEARLS IN MUSSEL SHELLS

One Thousand Men are Raking the Shells from the Waters of the Stream Between Terre Haute and Mouth of the Wabash.

Boats, Rakes and Cooker, at Cost of $40, is All a Fisherman Needs—Stories of Valuable Pearls Found by Hoosier Searchers.

Towns Are Pearl Mad.

Layers of Mussel Shells.

Sold Pearl for $690.

Thousand Fishermen on Wabash.

Buyers Are Speculators.

Interest in the Industry.

Dumped Into Warm Water.

Author's collection.

rakers would close the scoop and bring up their catch. On average, three to twelve shells were caught in each load.

The mussels were then hauled ashore. They were placed in water warm enough to cause the shell to open but not hot enough to spoil the meat. The pearls were dug out and then graded. Those considered imperfect or misshapen were called slugs and sold for a much lower price. Well-rounded pearls fetched the best prices. The meat was retained and often sold to restaurants. The shells were sold to dealers for buttons or other uses.

Agents for eastern pearl dealers made regular stops along the Wabash, buying up the best product. For a period, a Parisian dealer had a representative stationed permanently in Vincennes. Prices depended on the size and quality of the pearls of course. A fairly typical exchange was the six pearls harvested by a riverboat captain in Terre Haute named Sam Shewmaker in 1907. The large pearl sold for $100, while the five smaller ones were valued at $20 each. The largest Wabash pearl may have been the one harvested south of Terre Haute by a man named Leo Bouchner. It was over an inch in diameter and weighed nearly fifty grains. It was thought to have sold for almost $2,000.

The "Pearl Rush" was short-lived. By 1910, it was all but over, as the mussel population was decimated by overharvesting.

There was another group of searchers around Terre Haute called ragpickers. A local reporter noted that most Hauteans did not have the "remotest idea as to the number of men, women and children who earn a livelihood by picking up rags, paper and junk of all kinds." These were life's scavengers, whose days were a search for those things unwanted by others. The discardings of their "betters" were sometimes the only things standing between ragpickers and empty stomachs.

Ragpicking was often a family affair. It was not unusual to see parents and children on their rounds. They would start early, clad in the ragged clothing saved from previous outings. The first stops were usually the alleys in the business districts, where they eagerly pounced on items swept out by storekeepers. Then it was on to the neighborhoods, where their cries of "Any rags today, any bones, any bottles?" echoed through the streets. Housewives or maids would often scurry out with offerings.

There was a definite hierarchy among ragpickers. At the top were those who had a cart pulled by mules or horses. They could move quickly through neighborhoods, and their wagons could hold much more "junk." Next came those with two-wheeled carts. These ragpickers provided their own horsepower as they pushed or pulled their laden carts. At the bottom were those who could only afford burlap bags to carry their more meager gleanings.

Their rounds completed, ragpickers would haul their loads to the "junk houses" along the Wabash. Paper, pasteboard boxes, bottles and metals like zinc brought the highest "payday." With the few coins they earned, they would buy food (or sometimes liquor) and head home.

Taylorville was home for many ragpickers. To call Taylorville a slum was to give it higher praise than it deserved. Located on the west bank of the Wabash, it was home to the poorest of the poor. It was a shantytown that had sprouted near the Terre Haute city dump. Homes were often built of any scraps of wood or metal that had washed up along the banks. Malnutrition and disease shrouded every house.

Ragpickers often had sidelines. Running gambling games like dice or poker added a few coins to their pockets. Some ventured into Terre Haute to do shoeshines or pick up menial jobs. Those with musical talents would play fiddle or harmonica at dances or busk in the streets.

Within the ragpicker world were those who stood out for various reasons. One man was known as the "King of the Ragpickers." He was a quiet middle-aged man, but a big man of great strength. He eschewed any cart or conveyance. Instead, he lashed two large coffee bags together and draped them over his powerful shoulders. It was said he could carry as much on his back as any cart. His home was a "hovel over near the 'dump' in Taylorville." Word among his fellows was that all his meals came from scrounging food thrown out by restaurants. His clothes were those found in the streets. His only expense was coal oil for his lamp. This led many to believe that he had a gold cache hidden in his home. He was a man of great mystery. What had brought him to his current state was the subject of speculation among his peers. He kept entirely to himself and never mingled with others.

Then there was the Preacherman Ragpicker. He was a two-wheel cart man who was seen everywhere. His warbling of gospel songs mixed with the "any rags" cries of other pickers along the streets of Terre Haute. On Wednesday nights and Sundays, he donned his Prince Albert jacket to go out and spread the word. Where he got the fancy double-breasted, knee-length cutaway jacket popularized by Queen Victoria's consort was a mystery. He must have picked it up somewhere on his rounds and wore it as he set out to "snatch brands from the fires of hell" before it was too late.

To Be Free and Black in Terre Haute

William Clark was a "tonsorial artist." He was also a free black man who spent most of his life in Terre Haute. As such, he was a walking history of Terre Haute's black population prior to the Civil War. He spoke of that history to a reporter from the *Terre Haute Evening Gazette* in 1893.

There were twenty "Negroes" in Vigo County in 1820, and most lived in Terre Haute. That population would begin to grow with the formation of three free black farm settlements. The first was the Lost Creek Settlement. Like with many other settlements, the early pioneers were escaping from North Carolina and "restrictions imposed on them by state and local governments." Slave owners were always wary of free blacks, as they feared their freedom would lead to unrest among the slave population. In North Carolina, free blacks were treated as outcasts. Unlike many other such settlements that were aided and encouraged by Quakers, there appears it had little influence on the Vigo County settlements.

Bowen Roberts was sent from North Carolina in 1827 to scout out suitable places for settlement. Roberts was taken by what he saw in Lost Creek Township. As it was still government land, it could be purchased at a good price on credit. They would not have to try to purchase land from white owners, who would likely be reluctant to sell to "coloreds."

Bowen's refrain that in Lost Creek "fat hogs are roaming the forest with knives and forks in their backs" was all the encouragement his brethren needed. Many of the new settlers became very successful. The Roberts, Anderson and Stewart families became community leaders. Dix Stewart accumulated nine hundred acres of farmland that he was later to divide among his sons. Two other settlements, Underwood and Burnett, were founded in the 1830s.

Education was of paramount importance to the settlers. A school and church were founded in Lost Creek in 1835. William Clark attended the school as an adult for six months, the only formal schooling he ever had. His teacher was a man named Gilbert Saulter, whom Clark always remembered.

By 1840, Vigo County had a black population of 425. Most lived in the rural settlements, but there was a growing urban population too. The city folks worked at various jobs, in meatpacking and construction particularly. Barbering was always a profession seemingly dominated by black men. William Clark was among several "artists of the steel blade" in Terre Haute. Cutting hair was just a minor part of their trade. They spent much more time giving shaves with a straight razor. As now, barbershops were places people gathered, and barbers like Clark were among those most in the know about what was happening in town.

One of Clark's one-time partners was Edward Roye, a man who led a fascinating life. The son of former slaves, Roye was a very bright man and had a head for business. He advertised his tonsorial parlor and bathhouse with a seventy-nine-foot tall barber pole. Colonization of free blacks was a hot topic in Indiana, and Roye, though initially opposed to colonization, began to think of emigrating. His first inclination was to move to Haiti, and he began to learn French at Ohio University. A fellow student suggested he think about moving to Liberia.

After the death of his wife, Roye sailed to Liberia in 1846 with a load of trade goods. He was thirty-one. He became the leading businessman in

Liberia, running an import/export business. He soon became the richest man in that West African nation. He was attracted to politics and served a term in the Liberian House of Representatives and as chief justice of the Supreme Court of Liberia. In 1870, he reached the pinnacle of his political aspirations when he was elected Liberia's president. Unfortunately, Liberia's economy was in shambles, and there was growing unrest among native tribes. Roye had the Speaker of the House arrange a loan from Great Britain, but under very severe terms. There was an uproar, and after a trial exonerated the Speaker, he was murdered as he left the courthouse.

Roye was driven from office by a coup in 1871. A mystery still surrounds Roye's death in 1872. Some believe that he was killed, while others say he drowned while trying to board a British ship. Coincidentally, he died on Lincoln's birthday.

Bishop William Paul Quinn came to Terre Haute in 1837. Quinn was born in Calcutta, India, the son of a Spanish father and Egyptian mother. A Quaker missionary converted him to Quakerism, and Quinn adopted an English name. After immigrating to the United States, he converted to the African American Episcopal Church, the first independent black denomination. He established the Allen Chapel AME Church in Terre Haute in 1837. The church became a focal point of the black community. Among its ministers was Reverend Hiram Revels, who became the first African American U.S. senator when he was elected from Mississippi during Reconstruction.

The church was also a vital link in the Underground Railroad in the so-called western line. Fleeing slaves would come up from the Evansville area and make stops in Vigo County. The free black settlements were also important stopovers. John Underwood was once accosted by a group of slave catchers for his role in helping escaping slaves. Fearing that they were about to harm him, he gave the secret Masonic sign. Being fellow Masons, they left him alone.

By 1850, Vigo County had the second-largest black population in the state with 725 black residents, trailing only the Quaker-dominated Wayne County. There were also African Americans who were not free. Indiana law allowed indentured servitude, in which a person could sign an indenture binding them to another person for up to ninety-nine years for a "fee." In effect, it allowed de facto slavery. At least two wealthy Terre Haute white men had indentured black servants. "Henry, a poor Negro boy," was indentured by a Mr. Condit. A Mr. Chunn "paid [$320] for the service of a Negro man for eight years."

Of course, after the Civil War all black citizens in Terre Haute were legally free. But as in other areas, their condition can be best described as separate but not equal.

A Flag Burning in Terre Haute

Twenty-seven mostly drowsy students filed into the classroom for their 8:00 a.m. freshman English class at Indiana State University. It was Friday, April 14, 1967. Many only had thoughts of what they were going to do over the weekend, or that the semester would thankfully soon be over. A female student approached the instructor's desk. When she turned away, her classmates noticed that she had placed a spool of thread holding a small American flag and a book of matches on the desk. The scene aroused the sleepy students as they realized what was happening and wondered if the instructor would take the dare.

Scott Chisholm was a thirty-one-year-old Canadian in his fourth year as an English instructor at the university. He was known as an excellent instructor whose teaching methods were innovative and compelling. But some in the administration considered him controversial. They thought he used "sensationalism" to spur his students to "intellectual inquiries." To them, he was too radical, like he was some kind of beatnik or hippie.

They were also not happy that Chisholm and a fellow instructor had opened a coffeehouse (Chisholm was a child of the Beat movement) just north of campus called the Tin Ear. Chisholm saw it as an "after hours intellectual meeting place." It sold coffee and pizza and brought in bands from around the state. To some administrators, it was a breeding ground for radicals, especially when it hosted "anarcho-pacifist" black poet Joffre Stewart. Stewart was a committed radical who was mentioned in Allen Ginsberg's seminal Beat poem "Howl" ("big pacifist eyes sexy in their dark skin"). During his performance, Stewart allegedly tore up a small paper U.S. flag. It was later reported that there was no evidence that a flag burning took place. Chisholm was out of town on the day of Stewart's appearance.

The goatee-ed Chisholm walked into classroom. The next fifty minutes changed his life. During the previous class, Chisholm's intention had been to teach his students the differences between "the 'concrete' and 'abstract' aspects of language." He told them that an object could indeed be viewed only as an object (the concrete) without also burdening it with its symbolic (abstract) meanings. Using the example of a leftist French protester who burned an American flag, he cautioned his class that it was "important to differentiate between the symbolic implication of the act from the object destroyed." In this case, the protestor was burning not only the object but also the symbolism for which it stood.

But he stressed to his students that "any man could burn any flag so long as it is understood that he is not attacking the abstract value for which the flag stands." Most of the class seemed to understand the point he was making, but some did not or refused to accept the concept.

Chisolm looked at the class, reached for the matches and flag and set it alight. As it was eaten by the flames, he turned to the students. "This is not to be misconstrued as an unpatriotic act, because I am not herein involved with abstract questions about the values of my government [obviously the Canadian-born Chisolm now identified as an American], about its foreign policy, or about its actions." Pausing, he continued, "I am not attacking the principles for which it stands, nor am I making a political comment about democracy."

Instead, he reiterated what he had told the class previously. It was a concrete object that was smoldering in his hand—just a stick and a piece of cloth, "not my country or its principles." Chisolm put the flag in a sink in the classroom and continued his lecture. None of the students objected to the "lesson" during the remainder of the class. There were no protests or outcries at his deed. That would soon change.

Within forty minutes after the end of class, an angry parent was bellowing at ISU vice president Charles Hardaway. She reported that her daughter had witnessed a flag burning in her English class and was very upset. Hardaway called President Alan Rankin to inform him of the call and said he had asked Dean Richard Gemmecke and Professor George Smock, Chisolm's department head, to investigate the incident. Rankin also asked that the college's attorney check into Indiana's flag burning laws.

Interestingly, Chisholm was not contacted immediately about the incident. Instead, administrators first searched out students who had attended the class. Professor Smock met briefly with Chisolm at 11:00 a.m. and reported that he did not consider the incident serious enough to "warrant any immediate action."

Fearing that the media might beat him to it, President Rankin called Indiana governor Roger Branigan to tell him of the incident and report that the college had already begun an investigation. Branigan did not take it well. Rankin was right to be worried about the media. Shortly after the call to the governor, reporters were on the story. With the news out, Branigan issued a statement Friday evening saying, "I am heartsick that such an outrage would occur at such a fine university." It only took twenty-four hours for the word to rapidly spread, as stories appeared in Indiana newspapers and across the country.

Damascus Captures Preakness . . . Cubs Demolish Dodgers
500-Mile Race Has Full Field . . . Sycamores Win Two . . . *Details in Sports*

THE TERRE HAUTE TRIBUNE-STAR

★ COMPLETE WIRE SERVICES OF THE ASSOCIATED PRESS AND UNITED PRESS INTERNATIONAL ★

Vol. 37, No. 12. Section 1. Terre Haute, Ind., Sunday, May 21, 1967. FINAL Eight Sections —102 Pages. 25 CENTS

BOARD FIRES FLAG BURNER

Teacher Had Been Warned By Trustees

Scott Chisholm, 31, a Canadian born English teacher who publicly burned an American flag in front of members of his freshman English class April 14, was fired Saturday by the Board of Trustees of Indiana State University.

In announcing the board's decision, Dr. Wayne Crockett, president of the board, termed Chisholm's act "a display of poor judgment, and one which the hearing committee deemed unprofessional." Crockett also noted that the discharged university instructor "disregarded an admonishing letter sent him on March 1," nearly three weeks before the flag burning incident.

Crockett said the board, "realizing the gravity of its action, has accepted the recommendations of the special faculty hearing committee and President Alan C. Rankin" in regard to the dismissal.

SCOTT CHISHOLM

Average Speed of 33 Cars Over 164 MPH

By DALE BURGESS

INDIANAPOLIS (AP) — The 33-car field for the 51st running of the 500-mile race May 30 was filled to overflowing Saturday at a record average of 164.024 miles per hour. The old mark was 160.251 m.p.h. last year.

There will be one more qualifying session Sunday in which a car still can make the lineup by replacing one of the earlier runners with a faster 10-mile average.

Middle East War Imminent—Thant

By WILLIAM N. OATIS

PRESENT STUDY GRANT—Kenneth Levin, center, presents a fellowship grant to Sister Mary Jean of St. Mary-of-the-Woods in behalf of the Jewish congregation here for study of Jewish history at Hebrew University, Israel. Chuck Stransburg Photo.

Ground War, Air Battles Growing in Deadliness

By EDWIN Q. WHITE

Body of Young Woman Found In Car Trunk

MS Volunteers March Tuesday

House Votes to Curtail Participation Certificates

By JOSEPH R. COYNE

Indiana's Penal System Is Held to Be Archaic

Sen. Bayh Scores Victory in Defeat

By HOWARD STEVENS

SIX IN FAMILY FOUND SLAIN

The Weather

Inside Today's TRIBUNE-STAR

Article appearing the day after the flag burning. *Author's collection.*

Smock, Hardaway and Rankin met in the afternoon. Again, Smock said that he could not recommend dismissal but was tasked with writing a memo seeking to suspend Chisholm pending a hearing. It seems likely that Hardaway had already made up his mind. When Hardaway met with Chisholm later in the afternoon, he refused to let the instructor give his side of the story, saying he must wait for a hearing. When Chisholm asked to speak with Rankin, he was told that the president was in a meeting and would not meet with him until faculty had been notified and a special faculty committee was formed.

Word spread quickly through Terre Haute. Chisholm received death threats, and outraged "patriotic" groups howled for his dismissal; some wanted him deported. It was a fevered period in Terre Haute. It was partially fueled by the longstanding "town/gown" divisions that were strong in the city. A local radio station continued to push for action against the unpatriotic acts of a liberal professor. The controversy also put the Tin Ear under the spotlight. There was increased surveillance of the coffee shop, and it was closed for a period, supposedly for a building code violation. Advertisements for the Tin Ear emphasized that it was "still here" and touted that it sold pizza. All this even though Chisholm had reportedly divested himself of his ownership in the club before the flag burning.

A faculty committee was formed to conduct a hearing on the case. Its head was J. Robert Constantine, a highly respected history professor. The hearing date was set for April 25. At Chisholm's request, Hardaway presented him with a written summation of the specific charges against the instructor. It was given to Chisholm on April 23.

Hardaway's memo stated that Chisholm was charged with "unprofessional conduct" for burning the flag. While giving lip service to academic freedom ("a teacher is entitled to freedom in the classroom"), Hardaway's true feelings were reflected in his belief that a teacher should not introduce "questionable and repugnant matter not related to his subject." Obviously, Hardaway did not see the difference between concrete and symbolic as Chisholm did. Hardaway did not supply a copy to the faculty committee before the hearing. They were unaware of it until Hardaway read it into evidence at the hearing.

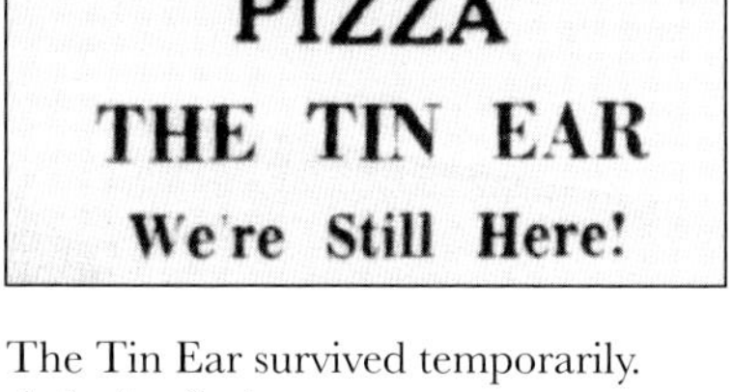

The Tin Ear survived temporarily. *Author's collection.*

On the day of the hearing, it was agreed per Chisholm's request that the hearing be closed, a verbatim transcript be made and only one witness at time be questioned. And then, in a rather Kafka-esque decision, the committed denied Chisholm's request that a member of the American Association of University Professors be present. The reason given was that it was a closed hearing.

Many of Chisholm's supporters felt he had been set up by certain members of the university administration. At a faculty wives dinner a week before the flag burning, a senior administrator told the group about the Joffre Stewart incident and predicted, "Well, I guess that's the end of the line for him [Chisholm]." That same administrator also had "very close relatives" attending Chisholm's classes.

The committee interviewed students in the class. Most stated that they did not see the burning as an unpatriotic act. Charles Adams stated that Chisholm had made it clear he was burning the flag as a symbol and that this did not reflect his views of the United States. Another pointed out, "It did not bother me that much because he explained the reason he did it."

Certainly, there was no evidence of a coordinated administration "conspiracy" to oust Chisholm, but the flag burning provided a sort of collective "Will no one rid me of this meddlesome priest" moment.

Chisholm wasn't the only Indiana teacher dismissed because of the flag burning. A Bloomfield English teacher named Patricia Reilly was fired because she reportedly "condoned" Chisholm's teaching method. It took only a few minutes for the Bloomfield School Board to dismiss her (without a hearing) when a parent accused her of being "a liberal with preconceived ideas" who "led our children to believe in freethinking." The parent was seconded by the local American Legion Post. Evidently, the Bloomfield School Board certainly did not want children to think for themselves. Who knows, it might have turned them into Commies or something.

The Chisholm case became an immediate *cause célèbre* among the academic community across the country. The June edition of *Phi Delta Kappan*, a professional journal for educators, carried a story on the case. The very pro-Chisholm article was obviously sparked by Chisholm colleagues. The September issue of the same publication saw the previous article as a "rush to judgement" and decidedly supported the administration's actions. However, the official motion by the ISU branch of the American Association of University Professors found fault with the administration's handling of the case, though not for its dismissal of Chisolm. It also called for further investigation "of the possibility that in the whole matter Scott Chisholm was 'set up' with the overt intent and for the purpose of placing him in a position in which he might be discharged."

The issue was still being discussed three years later when the American Association of University Professors' *AAUP Bulletin* looked back on the controversy. It concluded that ISU had indeed violated academic freedom protections. The general tenor was that this would not have happened if ISU was a "real university" like Harvard and other academic institutions. And this was not the first time ISU had egregiously caved to public opinion. When it was Indiana State Normal, it fired its most distinguished faculty member, John Schlicher, in 1918 simply because he pointed out that "not all Germans were bad." (See the author's "Holding a Course: Professor John J. Schlicher's Dismissal from Indiana State Normal" in the March 1992 *Indiana Magazine of History* for more on this story.)

Fortunately, the controversy did not hinder Scott Chisholm's career. He went on to teach at several colleges and earned a reputation as a fine poet. He did not look back on his time in Terre Haute. He resolutely refused interview requests to talk about the flag burning incident until his death in 2013.

Select Bibliography

Innovation

The Skies Above Terre Haute

Argosy. September 1961.

Johnson, Harry. Interview. Paul E. Garber Papers, Accession 1991-0063, National Air and Space Museum, Smithsonian Institution.

Terre Haute's Tornado and Flood Disaster, March 23–30, 1913. A pamphlet published by the *Terre Haute Star.*

Terre Haute Tribune. August 7–8, 1910.

The Natural-Born Mechanic

Peterson, D.D. "Gus' Aeroplane 1913." *Vintage Airplane,* September 1978.

Sullivan Daily Times. September 8, 1914.

Sullivan Democrat. May 27, 1915.

Sullivan Union. June 5, 1913.

Terre Haute Tribune. June 19, 1913.

Soda Pop's Pop

Terre Haute Saturday Evening Mail. December 29, 1894.
———. July 17, 1897.
———. March 24, 1894.
Terre Haute Weekly Gazette. October 13, 1881+.

Sportin' Life

Garfield Olympians

Bell, Gregory. *The Longest Leap*. Anoka, MN, 2018.
Lovellette, Clyde, and Lew Freedman. *The Story of Basketball Great Clyde Lovellette*. Indianapolis, IN: Blue River Press, 2015.
Marannis, David. *Rome* 1960: *The Olympics that Changed the World*. New York: Simon & Schuster Audio, 2008.
Terre Haute Tribune Star. August 21, 1955.

Four-Cornered Racetrack

Leehrsen, Charles. *Crazy Good: The True Story of Dan Patch*. New York, 2008.
Terre Haute Saturday Spectator. August 2, 1919.

Wooden, Walker and Winning

Davis, Seth. *Wooden: A Coach's Life*. New York: St. Martin's Griffin, 2015.
Klueh Family Scrapbooks, Indiana State University Archives.
Terre Haute Tribune. February 22, 1947.

Prizefighting: "Thugs and Murderous Toughs"

Terre Haute Weekly Gazette. April 29, 1886.
———. December 30, 1880.
———. June 10, 1886.

DISASTERS

Sandford's Month of Terror

McCormick, Mike. "Explosion Rocks Sandford." *Terre Haute Tribune Star*, January 12, 1997.

Terre Haute Tribune. January 20–April 27.

The Home Packing Explosion

Terre Haute Saturday Spectator. January 12, 1963.

Terre Haute Tribune. January 2, 1963.

———. January 3, 1963.

———. March 9, 1967.

ARTS AND LETTERS

The Miniaturist and the Diva

Ball, Susan W. "Woman's World: Amalia Kussner Coudert." *Terre Haute Saturday Spectator*, June 10 1911.

Coudert, Amalia Kussner. "The Human Side of the Tsar." *Century Magazine* 72 (1906).

Erdman, Andrew L. *Blue Vaudeville: Sex, Morals and the Mass Marketing of Amusement, 1895–1915.* Jefferson, NC: McFarland & Company, 2007.

McCormick, Mike. "Artist's Talent Was Miniatures." *Terre Haute Tribune Star*, March 27, 1997.

Terre Haute Saturday Spectator. July 27, 1891.

———. March 2, 1907.

Terre Haute Tribune Star. "Suratt Beautiful, Enigmatic." October 10, 17, 1995.

Hautean Hollywood

Terre Haute Tribune. April 27, 1913.

———. June 13, 1915.

———. June 20, 1915.
———. June 27, 1915.

We'll Make You a Star, Kid

IMDb Database. "Billy Lee." https://www.imdb.com/name/nm0496889.
Terre Haute Saturday Spectator. July 17, 1940.
———. June 6, 1940.
———. October 27, 1934.
Van Nuys Reporter. December 20, 1934.

AWFUL CRIMES

A Lynching on the Wabash

Logansport Journal. March 1, 1901.
Terre Haute Tribune. February 27, 28, March 3, 1914.

Flat Iron Murders

Terre Haute Star. March 16–17, 1915.
Terre Haute Tribune. March 17, 1915.
Vernie Lewis Records, Indiana Archives and Records Administration.

Death Cry of the Gypsy

Demetro John Records, Indiana Archives and Records Administration.
Terre Haute Star. May 6, 1914.
Terre Haute Tribune. May 4, 1914.

In Times of War

"One of Those Uncommon Geniuses"

Fort Harrison, Vigo County Historical Society Archives Center.
Sugden, John. *Tecumseh: A Life*. Bridgewater, NJ: Paw Prints, 2008.

Camp Harrison POW Camp

Camp Harrison POW Camp, Vigo County Historical Society Archives Center.
New Albany Weekly Ledger. March 26, 1862.
Terre Haute Daily Wabash Express. March 24, 1862.

The Lurking Spy

Castleman, John Breckenridge. *Active Service in the Confederacy and Spanish War*. Bellevue, WA, 2015.
Thompson, Stephen A. "Soldiers of Long Odds." Illinois State Historical Society History Symposium. Eastern Illinois University, March 27, 2014.

Strikes Three

America: A Land of Interchangeable Parts

Terre Haute Star. September 6, 1933.
Terre Haute Tribune. September 3, 5, 6, 1922.

Siege of Dixie Bee Mine

McCormick, Mike. "The Confrontation Battle at Dixie Bee Mine." *Terre Haute Tribune Star*, February 7, 2003.
Terre Haute Star. August 2, 3, 1932.
Terre Haute Tribune. August 1–4, 1932.

General Strike

Bailey, Gary. "The Terre Haute, Indiana, General Strike, 1935." *Indiana Magazine of History* (September 1984).

Bush, Donald. "The Terre Haute General Strike." Unpublished thesis, Indiana State University, 1958.

Thomas, Norman. "Hoosier Hitlerism." *The Nation*, September 18, 1935.

A TERRE HAUTE MISCELLANY

The Teacher and the Suffragette

Stanton, Elizabeth Cady, Susan B. Anthony, Matilda Joslyn Gage and Ida Husted Harper. Rochester, NY: S.B. Anthony, 1922.

Terre Haute Saturday Evening Mail. 1915.

Terre Haute Saturday Spectator. May 11, 1912.

Terre Haute Tribune. January 16, 1962.

Pearl Divers and Ragpickers

Indianapolis News. December 5, 1908.

Terre Haute Saturday Spectator. December 31, 1904.

To Be Free and Black in Terre Haute

Indiana Negro History Society Bulletin. "Lost Creek Settlement, Vigo County, Indiana" (March 1939).

Lyda, John W. *The Negro in the History of Indiana.* Terre Haute, IN [?], 1953.

Thornbrough, Emma Lou. *The Negro in Indiana Before 1900: A Study of a Minority*. Bloomington: Indiana University Press, 1993.

A Flag Burning in Terre Haute

AAUP Bulletin. "Academic Freedom and Tenure: Indiana State University" (March 1970).

Phi Delta Kappan. "The Chisolm Case" (June 1967).

———. "The Chisholm Case: Continued" (September 1967).

Statement of President Rankin on the Chisholm Case. Chisolm Files, Rankin Collection, ISU Archives.

About the Author

Tim Crumrin is an award-winning historian and author who has published more than fifty scholarly and general interest history books and articles. He is a summa cum laude graduate of Indiana State University, from which he holds degrees in American history and history of modern Europe. He taught at St. Mary-of-the-Woods College and served twenty-five years as a historian and director at Conner Prairie Museum in Fishers, Indiana.

His work has received awards from the American Association for State and Local History and a national Telly award for writing and directing the PBS documentary *Harvesting the Past*. In 2014, he was honored with the prestigious Lifetime Achievement in History Award, presented by the Indiana Historical Society.

His previous book, *Wicked Terre Haute*, was published by The History Press in 2019.

He lives in Terre Haute with his wife, Robin; daughter, Brynn; and four canine muses named Hildy, Hank, Huwie and Beau.